LAUGHING ALL THE WAY TO HEAVEN

By the Reverend Dr. Kim Strong

South Carolina United Methodist Advocate Press

Advocate Press

South Carolina United Methodist Advocate Press, Columbia, South Carolina
Copyright © 2024 by South Carolina United Methodist Advocate Press

First published in the United States of America in 2024
by the South Carolina United Methodist Advocate Press.

Library of Congress Cataloging-in-Publication Data
Laughing All the Way to Heaven
p. cm.

Cover photo: jakubgojda

ISBN 979-8-9883575-6-8

Dedication

I would like to dedicate this book to the many family members, friends and church members who made me laugh, cry, or ponder life in the last sixty-seven years. You have given me a plethora of thoughts and ideas, which resulted in this book. You also enriched my life immensely.

I also would like to dedicate this book to the love of my life, my wife, Margo. She often told folks, "He thinks he is a comedian." I suppose now we will find out if it is true.

Table of Contents

Holiday Reflections

Preface

Let me begin by thanking you for taking the time to pick up this book. If you are looking for a book that offers deep theological insights, this isn't it. The words justification, sanctification, and incarnation are not anywhere to be found in my book. I looked twice to make sure.

Instead, I prefer to talk about the things that happened to, and with, me as I travel the road to heaven laughing all the way. The first sixteen years of my life I attended a church where humor was not found. You were told every Sunday that Jonathan Edwards was right: God is holding your very soul in his hand, ready to happily send your sinning soul to hell. There is nothing there to laugh about.

I was blessed to find out that God loved me even when I am not lovely. As a Christian we should be the happiest, most joyous people on earth. We should be laughing all the way to heaven because of God's unending grace.

The stories I am sharing in this book are my life stories as a minister with forty-five years of experience. The names have been mostly changed to protect the innocent. Through the mountaintops and the valleys of life, I found laughter helped calm my soul.

When I was in high school at James F. Byrnes High School in Duncan, South Carolina, I was the wisecracker in class. I had a biology teacher who didn't like me interrupting her lectures with comments.

She asked me one day, "Mr. Strong, do you stay up at night thinking of funny things to say in my class?"

My answer just rolled off my tongue, "No, ma'am, they just come right to me."

That was the day I realized I wouldn't be a brain surgeon.

Despite the best advice of my teachers in seminary, I try to bring out all the emotions I can that are appropriate in church during a sermon. If I made you laugh several times and tear up once or twice, my job was done.

I would like to thank my wife, Margo, for making someone else's house a home and for listening to the same sermons for forty-five years. Through being together through a flood, a house fire, a tornado, numerous hurricanes, and raising two teenaged boys, we learned it's better to laugh than to cry.

I would like to thank the thousands of church members I've had who gave me great material and whose own life stories were testimonies of the power of forgiveness and love that Christ offers. I particularly want to thank the dozens of people who said, "You need to write a book." I hope you still feel that way after you read it!

God has a plan for our lives, and I think his intention for us is to laugh all the way to heaven. I hope you will join me.

—*Kim Strong, March 2024*

Introduction

As a pastor, I try to use humor in my sermons. Sometimes they were downright funny. Other times they were funny, but not on purpose. My wife often tells folks, "He thinks he's a comedian." I found the ministers who can't laugh at themselves and the foibles of life are usually not in the ministry long.

The following is a story about a church that takes laughter to another level. I hope it evokes a chuckle or two from you.

Newsweek magazine published an article not too long ago titled "Giggles for God." The story was about a new theological movement that started in Toronto, Canada. Six nights a week, a church there opens its doors to any who will come to share in a time of laughter. No jokes are told, or anecdotes shared. They found that laughter by itself was contagious. A few people would start laughing, and soon the entire church was literally rolling in the aisles. More than one hundred thousand people and seven thousand members of the clergy have visited this church to learn the process and carry it back to their home churches around the world.

Perhaps you have the same thought I had: those Canadians sure are strange people! As I read the article, however, I began to see the biblical background and significance of what laughter is supposed to be for a Christian. If a Christian cannot be joyful and learn to laugh, who can? We are the only ones who should always have something to laugh about.

Dr. Charles Barrett was a retired professor of religion from Wofford College. He taught a course in college on the humor of Christ. Jesus was not exactly an early version of Johnny Carson, but he spoke in terms and used illustrations that were downright humorous to his listeners. Imagine a camel going through the eye of a needle. That was funny stuff to the people of first-century Palestine.

Is there anything more humorous than watching a pew full of people trying to stifle the giggles in the middle of a church service? How about at a funeral service? Weddings are notorious for the many funny things that can go wrong. I remember one groom at a service I was conducting who could not repeat his vows. I kept telling him what to repeat, and he kept messing it up. I finally gave him the *Book of Worship*, pointed to the page, and asked him to start reading the highlighted words. The bride thought it was funny, but her mother was not amused.

There are enzymes the doctors say are released into your system only through laughter. God has wired us in such a way that we can only function at 100 percent of our potential when we laugh. It's only natural, then, that church would be a place where people go to share joy and laughter as well as tears and fears.

Another professor I had at Wofford, Dr. John Bullard, often told us to never do two things as a minister. We were never supposed to go on *Jeopardy* and try to answer religious or biblical questions, and we were never supposed to try to tell a joke in a sermon. The irony in those two statements was not lost on me.

John Wesley, the founder of the Methodist movement, was an Anglican minister who had a muted sense of humor. Now the largest Anglican church in London often has more than two thousand people cram into their old sanctuary for a "laughing service" on a Sunday night.

Job wrote that "God will yet fill your mouth with laughter and your lips with shouts of joy." If Job could find something to laugh about, surely we can find some humor in our own situations in life.

So, the next time something funny happens in church, don't try to stifle your laugh. That's bad for your sinuses, anyway. Let it roll. Laugh out loud. Laugh till you cry.

I am sure laughter brings a smile to our creator's lips and a snarl to our tormentors.

Chapter 1
How I Became a Character

In The United Methodist Church when a ministerial move is in the works, the prospective church and pastor have what is called an introductory visit. This sometimes becomes a high-pressure event where the church members and the pastor and family look each other over and decide if this is a marriage made in heaven or one made somewhere else.

The minister tells the church a little bit about themselves and their achievements, and the church tells the prospective pastor what they are looking for in their next minister.

The role of the superintendent is to act as a facilitator, making sure things stay on an even keel and no embarrassing questions are asked. An example of such a question could be, "Pastor we see your church was averaging two hundred in service before you came and seventy-five now. To what would you attribute this?"

The pastor could possibly retort that the Asian flu was particularly bad last year, and he had one hundred twenty-five funerals.

He then could ask the church, "I see where you have not had anyone join the church for the last six years. I was wondering why?"

The reply from the church could be to blame the evangelism committee and the sermons of the last minister.

The superintendent's job is to avoid such questions at all costs.

A few years ago during an introductory visit, we all sat down and broke bread together. In the midst of the conversation, the superintendent pointed out that the last two ministers they had were certainly a couple of characters. She then told the committee she knew I would feel at home here and I would fit right in.

I was not amused. A character? Moi? Why in the world would she think such a thing about me? What have I done to be lumped into such an undistinguished category?

I thought about this long and hard and came up with some possible answers. First, it could be the beard. I have worn facial hair since I was twelve. Even if it got a little boost from my mother's eyebrow brush, I had a moustache. In the words of the late George Carlin, "See my beard, ain't it weird, don't be scared, it's just a beard."

I had worn my hair a little long when I was younger. Maybe it was my appearance when I was a young man.

I got the minister's book off the shelf and started to look at my fellow colleagues. Some of their pictures were downright scary. Next to some of them I look like a card-carrying member of the Republican Rules Committee. Maybe that wasn't it.

Maybe she was placing me in the club because of some of my well-known hobbies. I ride a motorcycle. Not just a motorcycle, a Harley-Davidson. I like to ride down the road with my gray hair flowing in the wind and bugs bouncing off my teeth. I have a Harley-Davidson tattoo on my right shoulder. A simple H-D. My wife says it stands for a hundred dollars, which is the least amount I have ever spent in a Harley store on a shopping trip.

Maybe she heard about me playing guitar in a rock band called the Purpatrators. The lead guitar player was a church member who served on the church board and recruited me to play. We played oldies stuff from the seventies on Saturday night and in the church praise band on Sunday morning.

Maybe it was because of the athletics I was involved in over the years. I coached sporting teams for several recreational organizations and officiated high school basketball for more than sixteen years. Putting on a striped shirt and calling a game in front of several hundred angry, jeering fans was great preparation for a career in the ministry.

I have arrived at the conclusion that I am considered a character because of the things I have not done. I never became stuffy or out of touch with real life. I've never adopted one personality in the pulpit and one outside the pulpit. I am what I am, for better or worse.

I never became cliquish, running with the in crowd to become politically viable in the conference of the church. My folks were the ones who sat in the top row of the auditorium during conference reading a book or catching up on the news with old friends.

I am not a prodigy. My grandfather or father were not United Methodist ministers and had no coattails upon which I could ride in my career. My father preached, but only to Mom and me and whoever else was within earshot when the news came on at night.

I am a character and proud of it. I don't look or sound like most other ministers. I go my own way, dress to suit me, live in the real world, and like it.

Just like God intended.

Chapter 2
Never Follow a Rental Truck Too Closely

Author's note: In forty-five years of ministry, my wife and I have moved four-teen times. We once moved three times while pastoring the same church. We found that liquor store boxes were the best boxes to move in. They're sturdy, come with inserts, and best of all, they are free. They also give you a good excuse should a parishioner see your car parked in front of a liquor store. I wrote this story after a difficult move having said goodbye to folks we spent seven great years with. I hope it explains why you should never follow a rental truck too closely.

The United Methodist Church has a most unique system of supplying their churches with pastoral leadership. After several months of secretive meetings, pastors and churches are informed around April 1 of where their new assignments will be and who their pastor will be. After a short introductory visit to the new church, the pastor and their family return home to pack up their worldly belongings.

Moving day for every pastor moving is the last Wednesday in June. The minister must be out of their old house by noon and in their new house by nightfall. In just a few short hours, they leave behind the life they have known for four, five, or more years and start all over in a new place with new people, a new house, and a new church.

There is something freeing about leaving some places. You can pack up all your troubles and leave them behind in a trail of dust. Whatever, or whoever, was driving you crazy in your last church is gone forever. Your ministerial slate, both good and bad, is wiped cleaned. All the goodwill and trust you built in your last church has to be earned again in your new home. The folks you won't miss are left behind, but they have a way of showing up in your new church in different bodies.

Packing up all you own is a cathartic event. You must decide what is really important to you, what you want to keep, and what you can't live without. We usually find at least one box that we never opened after moving the last time. Boxes marked "mementos" and "keepsakes" are safely and securely placed on the truck each move, or they ride snugly in the trunk of your car where you keep your valuables.

Moving day is a time of bittersweet memories and heart-racing anticipation. As I have grown older, moving has become less exciting and more laborious. I have followed seven ministers who were retiring on moving day. They usually started the moving process months before and just gently slid into retirement on moving day.

Saying goodbye has become harder as I have aged in time and ministry. I have learned that the friends we were going to stay in touch with have faded from memory or gone to be with Jesus. Despite good intentions, friendships are never as close or as lasting. New friendships are formed, bonds forged, and memories made.

Through this process I have learned to never follow a rental truck too closely. Chances are it is being driven by a person who has just said goodbye to one part of their life and is in the process of starting over somewhere new. They are driving a strange vehicle down the road alternating between tears and a smile, between yesterday and tomorrow.

We are never sure of how many moving days we will have in life. We all are assured of at least one more when we slide into eternal life. Life is what happens between those moving days, not the anticipation of the next moving day.

The secret is to be ready to meet your mover when your moving day comes.

Chapter 3
Getting Lost in the 21st Century

Author's note: The most misnamed device in the world is the smartphone. It occasionally makes me question my own intelligence. One of the handiest devices it has is the Maps program. When I got my first smartphone, however, they were still working the bugs out of that program. The following is a story of how far we have come in ten years and how much we now depend on our phones.

One of the first things the parishioners at my new church gave me after a move was a giant road map of their county. I love maps. I used to sit and stare at the maps of our state and country when I was in elementary school, daydreaming about one day visiting places on those maps that were far, far away.

When I joined the Harley Owners Group, after buying my middle-aged, crazy, nine-hundred-pound toy, they sent me an atlas of the United States with detailed road maps of every state. Even every Harley-Davidson store was marked on the map for my shopping pleasure.

With the advent of the smartphone, they have tried to make most maps obsolete. I have an app on my phone called Maps. You just type in the address of the place you want to go, and it comes up with directions for you. If you hit the right key on the phone, a female voice will come on and give you step-by-step instructions on how to find your destination.

This app is a cheaper version of a GPS, or a Global Positioning System. This thing will, in a way known only to God and the Homeland Security Administration, find you in your car and show you on your way to where you want to go. The voice provides you with an additional female voice in the front seat telling you where to go, when to turn, how far you are from your destination, and even how fast you are driving.

It should be foolproof.

It's not.

I remember well the first time I ever tried using the Maps program to find my way. My son Jon and I were looking for an outdoor shooting range in Mount Pleasant, South Carolina, to practice our aim with two handguns.

The program told me exactly where to turn. It was a dirt road. That didn't worry me very much because the Lowcountry is full of dirt roads. We turned and took my new Dodge Ram pickup truck down the road.

We noticed the road started becoming narrower and narrower. Soon, we had water on both sides of the truck. We discovered the dirt road was a hunter's trail through the swamps.

When the road ended, there was a locked gate and no dry place to turn around.

I suggested to my son we shoot the lock off the gate and go back on the paved road. He said that was a bad suggestion, and we went through the drainage ditch instead.

We blamed this experience on my misunderstanding the directions from that British lady who lived in my phone.

A few months later, my wife and I left South Carolina to travel to Winston-Salem, North Carolina, to visit a church member at the Wake Forest University Baptist Medical Center. Neither of us had ever been there before. We simply typed the address into the phone, pushed a button, got navigational directions, and left for the hospital.

We followed each turn precisely every time. We found Winston-Salem and started driving on the side streets. It carried us away from town into a residential neighborhood. We pulled up in front of a three-bedroom, two-bath ranch-style house, and it proudly announced: "You have arrived at your destination."

I know collections have been down in the local churches in the last couple of years, but could they have really downsized this much?

Our arrival coincided with my wife's announcement that nature was calling on line one. I got back on the highway, and we started driving toward the only two tall buildings we saw in the distance. Six miles later, we found the hospital pretty much on our own. By that time, my wife's leg muscles had cramped from keeping her ankles locked together that long that I thought she was going to have to be admitted to the hospital herself.

What I have learned from this is that a paper map in the hand is most of the time worth more than two GPS systems on the dash. No satellite in the sky can replace a bladder-bloated housewife in the front seat with a map. We found our patient, my wife found the nearest restroom, and we both found our way back to South Carolina.

We now just use our GPS app to find yogurt shops and wing joints. They don't put those places on a map, but they should.

Chapter 4
Always Choose a Doctor with Small Hands

Author's note: One of the things I have learned in retirement is you need a good calendar program to keep up with your doctor appointments. I get more phone calls from Walgreens than I do from old friends and family members. I love the doctor I have now. He doesn't tell me I'm fat. He gently asks me to lose some weight and help him out. I get the same requests from potential pallbearers. Following is a story I wrote some years ago that expressed how I viewed the medical profession then. My viewpoint has changed as my years have accumulated.

I recently had my yearly physical. It had been five years since my last yearly physical. I am not overly fond of doctors. Being a man, I never go to the doctor unless I either break a bone or sever an appendage. When I think of going to the doctor, pain sensors in my brain start firing off impulses, reminding me of the many ways they hurt me the last time I went to their office.

The doctor requires bloodwork, which means nothing to eat or drink after midnight. It means getting up and driving, sans caffeine, to the doctor's office to have my blood drawn. Without caffeine, I am sure I was a danger on the highway to every other driver trying to safely make it to school and work.

I remember vividly my physical exam when I entered the Air Force decades before. The nurse watched me walk in, took my pulse, smelled my breath, and declared me ready to go. I had met their three requirements.

Twenty years ago, I changed how I choose a doctor. I only go to female family practice doctors now. My theory is this: They had to work twice as hard to get through school as the male doctors did. They also are much prettier and have smaller, warmer hands. The smaller hands are always a good selling point after you turn forty and you have to start getting prostate exams.

My bloodwork came back fine except for my cholesterol. It was something between three hundred and three thousand. She tried to explain that my bad cholesterol was good, and my good cholesterol was bad. Maybe it was vice versa.

A good cholesterol reading used to be anything under two hundred forty. Then somebody at a large drug company looked at the charts and discovered if they made the good cholesterol cut-off two hundred instead of two hundred forty, they could sell medicines to one hundred million more Americans alone. Suddenly your doctor started giving you that "look" as they read your figures. They explained that if you wanted to live to make it back to your car you must swear to take these two prescriptions for the rest of your life.

I agreed. Anything other than a shot was good news to me. I took the prescriptions to the drug store, and they brought me two bottles of pills, slightly smaller than a horse suppository. I am supposed to take these daily with a large glass of fish oil and abstain from red meat until the next millennium. If I do all these things, my doctor said I will live another forty years.

After two weeks of living this way, I decided that living another forty years wasn't my goal in life. Enjoying life the next forty years was. God did not intend on my body living on vegetables, for he gave me canine teeth to tear and rip Angus beef with. Worrying about my cholesterol raised my blood pressure, which resulted in two more pills. It can be a vicious circle.

The secret is moderation. Always eat a small salad with dressing on the side before your pork barbecue sandwich, chili cheese fries, and chocolate cake are served. Always eat three servings of fruit every day, particularly if they are floating in a frozen beverage of your choice. If chocolate cake isn't your thing, try New York cheesecake with cherries on top. That is a great combination of fruit and dairy.

Always follow such a healthy meal with a short nap, or a long nap, if time allows.

I read recently that the average doctor dies at the age of fifty-seven. Get your exercise by going to their funerals and saying your goodbyes.

We all have a different amount of sand in our eternal hourglasses. Make the most of each grain of sand God has given you. When your time comes, your cholesterol level isn't going to matter much.

By the way, I've never heard any person on their deathbed say, "I wish I hadn't had that Big Mac last year."

I am proud to say I visit my small-handed doctor on a regular basis now. Her office is right beside this burger place that has food you could, and very well may, die for.

Chapter 5
Why Ask Why?

One of the joys of having a children's sermon is fielding the unexpected questions that kids will ask you in a church full of people. When the late Art Linkletter said, "Kids say the darndest things," he was right! Most of the questions that stumped me over the years were philosophical ones. I never stood up to conduct a children's sermon and was not nervous beyond reason.

My wife recently came home with a list of questions titled, "Why Ask Why?" They are slanted toward those of us who are adults but often think like a child.

For instance, why are there flotation devices under airplane seats instead of parachutes? It always made me concerned when the flight attendant would announce that you could use your seat for a flotation device and I was flying over Kansas. Was the pilot's sense of direction that bad?

Another example is the local 7-11 stores. If it is open twenty-four hours a day, three hundred sixty-five days a year, why do they put locks on the door? The next time you are in one, ask the clerk behind the counter why he has locks on his door. I bet he doesn't know.

Why do they put Braille dots on the drive-through menu at McDonalds, especially on the driver's side? I can better understand why they have them on the ATM machines, but on a drive-through? If you are so blind you have to use Braille to read, how did you find the drive-through to start with?

Other questions discussed were why do we drive on parkways and park on driveways? Why do they package hot dog wieners in groups of eight and the buns in groups of ten? The last question on the list asked, "If a cow laughed, would milk come out her nose?"

As we become older, our questions become more difficult and the answers more fleeting. Why God did you allow this to happen? Why do good people suffer and evil ones prosper? Why are some prayers answered so quickly and others seem not to be answered at all?

Those are the questions that matter the most as we get older. You can't Google those questions and get a quick answer. The questions we really want answered we are afraid to ask because we are fearful of the answer we may receive.

The great philosopher Forrest Gump once said, "Life is like a box of chocolates. You never know what you are going to get." We may not know the secrets of this world or even the right questions to ask. We just unwrap each day, like candies in a box, and take what each new day brings.

As we get toward the end of our lives, the question "why" is replaced by the question "when." When are things going to finally get better? When are people going to wise up and live better lives? When are the citizens of the world going to start loving our neighbors as we do ourselves? When is our time to die going to come?

Unlike the inquisitive child, our questions become less and less, but their answers become harder and harder.

Chapter 6
The Day You Know You Are Old

There has been an argument for the last fifty years about when life begins. The Supreme Court Roe v. Wade decision did not end the discussion; it merely facilitated it for another generation. I have no trouble with this argument because I believe life begins the moment God blesses the union of an egg and an opportunistic sperm and a new life is conceived.

At this point in my life, the bigger question for my generation is, "When do you become old?" The good folks at AARP sent me a free membership recently. I got my first one when I turned fifty some years ago. It came with a dozen brochures telling me all the places where I could use my card for discounts, including hotels, motels, restaurants, and airlines. I was pleased to get it since I love to travel.

Everyone is not so enamored to receive theirs. My wife, who is several years younger than I, turned up her nose at her card. She likes to point out that I married a much younger woman. A nearly blind, and obviously dumb, woman at a bank ten years ago thought I was her father. She has never let me live that down, and I am quite sure she won't. She has already ordered her tombstone to say, " Loving wife and mother ... and they thought I was his daughter."

What adds to the mystery of old age is this new concept of what middle age is. People now think middle age extends to sixty. That is true if you plan on living to be one hundred twenty. When faced with the math, you are forced to say that middle age is around forty. That means I am closing in on being three decades older than middle age. If fifty is the new forty, what is seventy?

In an effort to keep Social Security from failing, our friends in Washington want to extend the age at which you can draw your first check to the age of sixty-seven or beyond. That's assuming there is anything left in the coffers, which is a large assumption at this point in history.

I became a grandfather when I was fifty years old. I certainly did not feel old. I rode my Harley-Davidson Fat Boy to the hospital to greet the entrance of my grandson into the world. It's not my fault my son and his wife had children at such a young age. I acted as if fifty was the new twenty-one and lived to write about it.

Regardless of your chronological age, there comes a time when we all realize we have become old. For me it was the day I realized I had become the person I used to laugh about. When I was a young man and a young Christian, I used to make great fun of the minister at my home church. He was old and out of touch with the real world. He was set in his ways. He lived in the past and didn't understand what was happening in 1974. He had no dreams and some days acted as if he could not wait to retire. His decisions extinguished the Holy Spirit in our church. I wondered if he was even a Christian.

I can't believe the things that come out of my mouth occasionally. Phrases like "I've never done that before" and "maybe we should study that a little bit" flow from my aged tongue with regularity. I play in a praise band at my church, and this new praise music has me shaking my head every now and then. Music we played ten years ago now is outdated. I would much rather drive a bus full of senior citizens than a bus full of grade-school kids. The smell of Ben-Gay is better than the smell of dirty tennis shoes.

Yes, I am old and proud of it! With age has come wisdom. I know what I like and what I don't. I know what I can do well and what I have no business trying to do. I have become part of the dinner at 4:45 crowd. The rut I have spent nearly seventy years digging is called my life, and it hasn't been that bad. I have much more respect for my elders and great respect for that minister fifty years ago who stood by me in the toughest times of my life.

I am not middle-aged—I am old. And I plan to get older.

Chapter 7
Sending the Wrong Advertisement

I have spent more time on the highways and byways of life than most people. This has given me the opportunity to see a lot of things that are memorable and a lot of things that can't be forgotten. I have seen some very interesting bumper stickers and personalized tags over the years. I used to have a bumper sticker on my car that said, "My Boss Is a Jewish Carpenter."

This is the time of year when I have to make that dreaded trip to the Department of Motor Vehicles. I would not have to make this trip if I remembered to pay my taxes and tag fees early over the internet or even by the dinosaur we call the United States Postal Service.

However, I can always be counted on to be late. After much mumbling and grumbling, I pack my backpack with my iPad, a drink, something low-carb to munch on, and enough reading material to pass the three to four hours I know awaits me there.

While enjoying my few hours of peace and quiet there, I had the opportunity to memorize the personalized license tag chart. In South Carolina, virtually every organization in the state has a personalized license tag. Every school, civic organization, wildlife group, and fraternal organization has a tag you can put on your vehicle for an additional price.

South Carolinians like to personalize their vehicles. I have an Elks tag on my truck. It was fifty dollars cheaper than my college tag would have been, and the Elks needed the money.

The tag that gives me heartburn driving down the highway is the "In God We Trust" tag. It is not that I disagree with the statement. It's the driving habits of the tag's owner that often discredits the sentiment.

On my way to Charlotte the other day, I was cut off in traffic by the owner of one of those tags. He was doing at least eighty miles per hour and swerving in and out of traffic. He came within a foot of blasting a poor Carolinian (one without a personalized tag) in the rear before swerving abruptly in front of an eighteen-wheeler who laid down on the horn. The driver's response in the offending vehicle was to return a one-finger wave to the truck driver and speed off.

I took a little solace in the fact that the offending driver's car did not have a "Meet Me at Such and Such United Methodist Church Sunday" bumper sticker on it. However, on behalf of all of Christendom, I was embarrassed by his actions. I felt like passing the truck driver and making the sign of the cross out my window, but I figured he had already seen one finger too many that morning.

I long ago ran out of fingers and toes to count on the many times I have been cut off, run on the shoulder, or given the fickle finger of fate, and was amazed that they were owners of this tag. I have my own faults as a driver. I hug the center line, figuring I paid taxes on both sides of the road, so why not use both sides? I park my big, oversized truck in the middle of two parking places. I don't want dents and dings on my doors, and I have a hard time getting in and out of one parking space with that truck. I don't speed usually on the interstates, but I have a hard time doing forty-five on a four-lane highway. God never intended on us to drive that slow in a space that big.

My driving habits are one reason I never considered buying that tag. I did not want to reflect poorly on the message of the tag. Besides, if I lose my cool and say or do something stupid when I get mad at another driver, I just must apologize to God and my passengers, not to everyone in town who, no doubt, would have seen me do it or heard about it at the beauty shops, in-and-out stores, and other places of communication in town.

So if you buy the tag, God bless you. But drive as if you are not in a hurry to meet God today. The rest of us who have agnostic tags would appreciate it.

Chapter 8
Drop Kick Me, Jesus, Through the Goalposts of Life

One of the truths of life I have found is that you have very few real friends in life. We have many acquaintances. I have nearly eight hundred "friends" on Facebook. Many of these people I have not seen in twenty or thirty years. Some could not pick me out of a police line-up.

To say someone is your best friend indicates a level of friendship, trust, and love that is rarely seen anymore. The Internet has coined a phrase for this. It is called BFF, or best friend forever. A few people are lucky enough to have been blessed with such a friendship in life.

Ten years ago, my BFF died. He up and left this world on me way too soon. We both grew up in cotton mill towns in Spartanburg County. He was around ten years older than me, and we did not meet until I was twenty-five years old.

We were in seminary together at Erskine and later at Emory. Our relationship grew over the years, and he gradually became the older brother I never had.

His life was not perfect. He was on his second marriage when we met and had been raising his two daughters by himself until he met his next wife. He was the stepfather to her son, and they had a son together. His, hers, and ours became theirs. With a wife and four children, he left his first career as a photographer and entered school to become a minister.

In the late eighties, he suddenly became single again, and our home became his refuge from the judgmental eyes and ears of his parish. His life for the next ten years was very difficult until he met his last wife. I had the pleasure of marrying them in his church, and they enjoyed their few years together.

He was my golf buddy. When we were both in the same area, we played golf virtually every week at 7:30 on Wednesday morning. Winter or summer, we were out there for our four hours of therapy. In thirty years of playing golf, I beat him once. It was not about the competition; it was about the fellowship.

He preached a revival for me in several of my appointments. Once we went to play golf before the evening services and stopped at the local fast-food place and pigged out before returning home. When we walked into our house, we found the table set and a five-course meal waiting for us that my wife had prepared. We sat down together without uttering a word and proceeded to eat again. My wife was not the wiser.

His sermon that night was only eight minutes long.

When I bought a motorcycle in 2002, he went out and bought one also. I never knew he rode as a teenager. We rode to the beach with our wives and enjoyed ourselves until his knee replacement ended his days as a biker.

Ten years ago, as I was in the Los Angeles Airport returning from vacation, my cell phone began to ring. His wife called and said I needed to talk to her husband. He told me he was in the hospital and had been diagnosed with leukemia. He went to the emergency room with what he thought was a bug bite and turned out to have leukemia.

His last six weeks were hell on earth. High doses of chemotherapy left him weakened. He developed an infection that took him from this world on November 11.

We had often talked about what we were going to do in retirement. We had made a pact that if either of us won the lottery, we would buy two houses side by side on the ocean and retire there. We both loved Folly Beach, and he wanted to spend his last years resting there.

He had made many plans for what he was going to do. Dying wasn't in the plans. We often looked forward to the day when our responsibilities as a pastor would be over and we could relax and enjoy life. That never happened.

Many times since his death, when something good or bad happened in my life, I reached for the phone to call him. I wanted his advice, his counsel, or just to tell a joke or two.

As per his request, I preached his funeral. It was the hardest thing I have ever done in church. He asked for a special song to be played at his funeral.

With the bishop in attendance, we played "Drop Kick Me, Jesus, Through the Goalposts of Life." It wasn't traditional, but neither was he.

He was buried in the cemetery of his last church near Columbia. When his coffin was placed in his vault, I covered the top of it with sand I had brought from Folly Beach. I got it from under the pier where we used to walk and talk. I placed three golf balls in the crook of his arm in the coffin with him, just in case heaven has a course or two.

I still look forward to spending my retirement with him; it just won't be at Folly Beach. I don't look forward to the day I can relax and be happy. I have decided that now is that time. There are some things in life that should not be put off. Enjoying yourself and what life offers are two of those things.

Don't forget to thank God for your BFFs he has given you. You never know how long they will be with you.

Chapter 9
Why I Always Look Wrinkled

Author's note: I am a full-fledged baby boomer. I grew up in the sixties in the South. I went to segregated schools, worshipped in a segregated church, and even was seen by a doctor who had segregated waiting rooms. I remember segregated public bathrooms and water fountains. I remember the first African-American student I ever attended school with. Jerry Rice was his name, and he became a friend to every person in our school. Even as a child, I knew the world I lived in was not what God intended. The following is a story about my weird way of protesting racism.

One of my wife's pet peeves about me, and I am sure there are many, is that I will not let her iron my clothes. She always asks me if I need anything ironed, and I always tell her no. I tell her there is no reason in the world to put stiff, starched shirts on a lumpy wrinkled body. It's like putting a pig in a black tuxedo. When all is said and done, you still have a pig.

When I was in the Air Force, I would iron my own shirts each night before I went to bed. My nametag and cross and rank had to be just so. I worked for a colonel who would let it be known if it was not right. I put so much starch on my shirt I could stand it up beside the bed before I retired for the night. I could almost dive into it the next morning.

One time my wife got mad at me, pulled all my shirts and cotton pants out of the closet, and ironed and starched them all while I was gone. She knew it would upset me, but she had no idea why.

The real reason I didn't allow her to iron came back to light for me when we went to see *The Help* at the theater. This movie was the story of a young idealistic girl in Mississippi who wrote about race relations in the 1950s and

1960s in her state. The movie was told from the point of view of two dozen maids who had worked for White families for generations.

It was a moving film to watch. In a matinee of eighteen people, there were only two men. They had to wake the other guy up when the movie was over. I watched it all because it brought back childhood memories of having grown up in a segregated South that I had tried to repress.

My mother and father could not afford a maid. They both worked forty to forty-eight hours a week in a textile mill for their entire working lives. They worked opposing shifts, which meant my dad was home during the day, and they shared the housekeeping duties, including washing, cleaning, and cooking.

Each week, my mother would take her clean laundry, including blouses, shirts, and pants, to an African-American woman named Rosa Lee. Rosa Lee was an elderly lady, in her late sixties or seventies, which I thought was ancient then. She lived with her sister, whose name I can't recall.

It was an adventure to go to her house. She lived in a part of town I knew little about. Her house sat on the top of a hill with a long set of steps going to her front door. We would enter her home through the kitchen door. Her house had strange smells that ours did not. I learned later the smells were coming from what she was cooking. That was my introduction to soul food.

Each week my mother would take our laundry and pay her a few dollars. Rosa Lee was always nice to me and always took time to talk with me. Our laundry was always ready, always nicely ironed and starched and waiting by the kitchen door on hangers my mom had brought over earlier.

Down deep in the heart of a four-year-old, I knew something wasn't right about what was happening. My mother did not use the N-word in its common form. She called Rosa Lee and her sister ne-grees. I have never heard anyone else pronounce "negro" the same way. I knew that whatever she was trying to say, it was not a term of endearment.

I understand the capitalist system in our country. I know she was providing a service, and my mother used her service and paid her for it. It just did not feel right. Rosa Lee never made my mother a chocolate pie, like in the movie, but I bet she felt like it.

The Help brought back that same feeling in me I felt as a child.

I am ashamed to have anyone iron my clothes but myself. I was ashamed to see how African Americans were used and treated then, and the modern-day steam iron brings up those same feelings today.

So if you see me in a wrinkled shirt and pair of khakis pants, now you know why. It isn't that my wife and I don't have an iron. It is my form of protest of the racism that was, and still is, in our world.

Chapter 10
Being Bionic

Back in the golden age of television (when *Charlie's Angels* was the Number One show), I use to watch a program called *The Six Million Dollar Man*. It starred Lee Majors as an unfortunate test pilot whose plane nose-dived into the ground at five hundred miles per hour. Doctors replaced one eye, both arms, both legs, and who knows what else in between. He became the bionic man. His new abilities included leaping over cars, outrunning trains, and such.

It wasn't long before he was joined by the bionic woman, Lindsay Wagner. I don't recall how she became disjointed, but I am sure it was in a horrible accident.

Many of us today have become bionic people. I had folks in my churches who have more metal in them than a 1995 Chrysler. Hips are replaced with a device made of metal and plastic. Jack Nicklaus, the world's greatest golfer, had his hip replaced years ago and still played golf until he couldn't see his ball land anymore because of bad eyesight. I don't see most of my drives land either, but that's because I can't see through trees and under water very well.

My wife had her left knee replaced twelve years ago. She injured her knee when she was sixteen years old playing high school basketball. She went through three operations on the knee, countless injections, and various pain killers until she reached an age the doctors felt was adequate for a replacement. After three months of strenuous rehabilitation, she woke up one morning and her knee didn't hurt anymore. She has a new lease on life because she has regained mobility we felt may had been lost forever.

Doctors regularly give people new sight by transplanting corneas and removing cataracts. Kidneys and hearts are transplanted on a daily basis in hospitals across the land. Even hair transplants are possible now for the follicly impaired.

In 1997, I tried to catch a player who was falling in a church league basketball game. It was the least I could do because I was the one who was making him fall. He fell behind me but, on the way down, grabbed my left elbow and twisted it behind me until it was in front of the front of my chest. My arm was completely torn out of a socket, and the socket was broken off.

Three days later, when I decided it wasn't going to heal itself, I went to an orthopedic surgeon who put Humpty Dumpty back together again. Many crews and pins later, he semi-fixed me.

While it is amazing what doctors can do, Christians for centuries have been receiving transplants on a regular basis. Christ has given people new hearts and leases on life for more than two thousand years. He renews us in places doctors still can't reach. He renews our strength. He gives us peace in our hearts where stress and worry has resided for years. He gives us love when we thought love had left us for good.

I hope more people in our churches will receive a heavenly heart transplant. It's worth more than six million dollars!

Chapter 11
I'll Have Just a Byte

There are many first-time events in a person's life that they will remember forever. The first bike ride down the street. The first time you got up the nerve to steal a kiss from the person you were "going with." Graduations. Weddings. Births. Those are all special events in our lives.

I woke up this morning thinking about the very first computer I bought. It was a Radio Shack Color Computer 2. You had to hook it up to your television, and what little data you could save was saved on a cassette tape. The operating manual for this little piece of heaven was two inches thick. We had to enter the programs into the computer by typing them on the keyboard. One little mistake, and the entire program would not work. My wife and I spent six hours one night inputting a program that would count down from ten to one in different colors. We thought we were high-tech geniuses.

As computers became more powerful and less expensive, my interest in them grew more each year. I eventually started building my own. I spent $1,000 for component parts for a computer I could have bought for $600. There was much satisfaction when I would flip the switch and the whirl of the fan and hum of the hard drive excited my senses.

I am old enough to remember the first time I heard about the internet. A seer appeared on *The Today Show* and said that one day we would do the majority of our shopping online and emails would replace the U.S. Post Office. I scoffed at his remarks. Who wants to buy something you can't see and touch? Who really knows what happens to an email when you hit send? I sent messages friends claimed they never received via email. Did some guy named Chin Chan Chun in China get my email by mistake?

As usual, the experts were right, and I was wrong. I can't imagine now getting through a Christmas shopping season without the internet, my iPad, and FedEx. Between sites like Amazon and eBay, who needs to go out to the mall and wrestle with middle-aged women over the last sweater and slacks in the Myrtle Beach area? I simply go to the store's website, hit "add to the cart," pull out the old plastic money, and in two to three days FedEx or UPS delivers another soon-to-be present to my doorstep.

I now use Whitepages.com to find those lost addresses for persons I want to send a Christmas card to this year. If I am feeling cheap, I can just go to Facebook and send a free message to their Facebook page. No fuss, no muss, no stamp. Chances are, if I have not seen you in person or spoken to you on my smartphone, you won't be getting an actual card. I know my high-tech devices are in sync with each other when my phone sends me a text message telling me my computer at home has received a Facebook message wishing me a Merry Christmas.

I am expecting that in a few years the Santas at the malls will be replaced by a sixty-four-inch monitor. Santa will speak to our children from his desk way up in the North Pole via Skype. The children will be encouraged to send their Christmas list to Santa through text messages while Santa speaks to the group drinking a cup of hot chocolate surrounded by his happy elves. I am shocked some enterprising mall somewhere has not already done this. No long lines to see Santa, and no chance the children will find out it is not hot chocolate Santa is sipping on in that cup.

It's all just a matter of time.

Chapter 12
Three Vital Steps to Survive in the Ministry

Early spring is an interesting time of year for the Methodist Church. Ministers who wish to retire must let the bishop know by March of their plans. Each year, twenty or more ministers trade their vestments for a soft chair, hopefully with a view of the beach or the mountains. A few ministers will decide that the life of a minister is not for them, and they will leave the ministry for honest work elsewhere.

Just like the cycle of life, this is also the time of year when new candidates for ministry will stand before a committee or board and prayerfully answer their questions and hopefully be approved as new clergy. If things go well, in June at Annual Conference they will be ordained and two weeks later shoved out into the mission field we call the parish ministry.

As a supervising pastor, I had the responsibility of leading a dozen or so men and women through this long process. As their mentor, I was there to answer questions they may have and to impart what wisdom I have attained in forty-plus years of ministry.

Here is what I usually tell these nervous folks. First, develop the ability to be awakened from a deep and restful sleep at 6:30 on a Saturday morning to answer the phone. When you answer those calls, you must be able to speak in a clear, concise voice. You should loudly proclaim to the offending church member that no, I wasn't sleeping. I have been up since 4:30 reading my devotional books and praying for you and your family.

Do this even if you have no idea who he or she is or whether they have a family or not. This always impresses the person on the line who was wondering what time your 11 o'clock services start on Sunday.

Second, join the AAA auto club immediately. Your starting salary will make driving a newer model car impossible. You will be called out late at night and early in the morning. Rain, sleet, snow, and hundred-degree heat should have no effect on the dedicated minister. Your chances of having car trouble are directly proportional to how far apart your three- or four-point charge churches are located (i.e., see Walterboro District).

Third, even if you own the latest New International Version of the Bible, and read from it each Sunday from the pulpit, learn to pray in the King James language. Everybody knows that God places prayers made in such language at the top of his to-do list each day. Besides, it sounds very distinguished from the pulpit.

Finally, learn to completely memorize names and faces. This has been a great downfall of mine. I have a cousin by marriage in my family whom I have called Fred for years. His real name is Robert, but he looks like a Fred to me.

Such a poor memory can get you into lots of trouble really quick in the church. Pray your first appointment has a pictorial directory. Leave a copy in the bathroom and one beside your bed. Let it be the first thing you pick up in the morning and the last thing you put down at night.

This will not help you at Christmas and Easter when your twice-a-year folks show up, but it will get you through the other fifty weeks most of the time.

Other than that, you are on your own. I wish you luck and hope that one day you will retire and have an ocean or mountain view of your own.

Chapter 13
You Have Ugly Feet

Sundays after church and lunch have settled into a comfortable routine for my wife and me. We drag into the house, take off the Sunday go-to-meeting clothes, grab the iPad, and go to bed. After reading through a few state newspapers, I turn up the sound on the television and let the drone of the NASCAR race send me to sleepy land. There is nothing like the noise of forty race cars going in an endless loop to put me sound to sleep.

After the nap, we have a light supper, settle back onto the sofa, and watch Sunday night television. We conclude our peaceful evening by watching Desperate Housewives. It is a funny show, and it gives me untold sermon ideas for the next Sunday. Besides, God has been very good to Teri Hatcher!

One Sunday evening recently, the serenity of the evening was broken as my wife suddenly exclaimed, "You have funny-looking feet."

I immediately put down my popcorn and examined my feet for obvious flaws. Having found none, I replied, "What do you mean I have ugly feet?"

"Well, look at them," she said. "Your index toe is almost as long as your big toe."

After a second look, I was tempted to go and find the tape measure, but to keep peace I simply said, "The better to grip the floor with, my dear."

My wife has always pointed out the flaws of other people's feet. She also lets me know if a lady has pretty feet. She has foot envy. She wears size eleven shoes. At one time it was hard for her to find footwear that would fit. The overflowing closets of our house testify that shoemakers realized the plight of the metacarpally challenged and started making larger size shoes for women.

My opinion is that I have never seen a good-looking foot. Your foot is an engineering miracle. Something so small—well, usually so small—built to support a body so big. God obviously worked overtime on this project. If your feet become sore and hurt from the strains of its purpose, your whole body gets out of sort.

When you think about it, your feet are a very valuable thing. I remember my very first superintendent telling me how important it was to get my FOOT in the door. I lamented several times during my ministry about folks I wanted to give the left FOOT of fellowship to. I have always been taught to do the best I can and to put my best FOOT forward. I was never sure which foot that was, but I think it was my right one. Now I am not sure I have a right foot.

The foot is a holy part of the human body! The Bible clearly states that Jesus washed his disciples' feet. He didn't wash their face and hands. He got down on his knees and washed their feet, and I don't recall him telling anyone they had strange-looking feet. It would have definitely spoiled the moment, I'm sure.

The human foot supports not the human body, but it also supports the American economy. My wife often goes for a pedicure. She debates for days about which nail color would accent her wardrobe the best, and then she heads off for the salon to get her "nail" done. I walked by the salon in Wal-Mart the other day and there must have been fifteen women laid back in that place getting their toes painted. To my surprise, there was also one man there. They had a bench grinder and a chainsaw beside his chair. I guess he had not had his toenails trimmed in a while.

Considering all of this, it is clear to see why my feelings were hurt so badly by my wife's comment. Strange feet. She had been with me for thirty-five years. Had she been withholding the fact that my toes give her the willies? What is she going to tell me next? That back hair freaks her out? That I sing off-key in the shower? That my mouthwash isn't cutting it anymore?

It's not knowing what is coming next that worries me the most.

I find myself now staring at my feet and daydreaming. I think I will just buy more socks, wear them all the time, and be done with it.

Chapter 14
Anchors Away

For years the annual family vacation meant one thing: a trip to Myrtle Beach, South Carolina, better known as the Redneck Riviera. We would pack a week's worth of clothes, snack foods, and recreation items (i.e., golf clubs) and head out in the family truckster for the beach. Most of the time we traveled as an extended family. Grandparents, the two of us, and our two children and whoever they had talked us into bringing along would make our pilgrimage to the beach. We never seriously thought we would retire and move here, but we are glad we did.

We once had six teenaged boys with us on vacation. Never again. I threatened to send them all back, minus our two, if they did not quit putting sand, eggs, and cola into each other's beds. Things settled down, and everyone made it through the week.

In 1989, my wife and I decided we needed to get away on our own. We booked our first cruise on an unnamed cruise line. We had high hopes of having a great time until we arrived at the airport to catch our flight to Northern Cuba, also known as Miami. The man behind the airline ticket counter told us he did not know our ship was back in service after the big fire and all they had a few months ago. That wasn't encouraging.

We arrived late in Miami and were whisked away to our awaiting ship. It did not look like I thought it would. If looked as if it had been renovated by the Polish Navy. It was crude, dirty, and still smelled a little like smoke.

Our cruise was not what we had planned. The ship was tossed about until my wife had the beginnings of seasickness. I rushed her to the casino, bought her a margarita, and gave her two dollars of nickels. She sipped her drink and played the slot machines for four hours until she had lost her two dollars.

We went snorkeling the next day and she backed into a red hot, flesh-burning piece of coral. I came up from snorkeling and saw her raising up the back of her swimsuit and showing her behind to a strange man. She thought something was still biting her backside, and the man thought it was his lucky day.

It was almost twenty years before we got on a cruise ship again. My, how things have changed. We love cruising now. Where else can you get away from your phone, the internet, your work, and the people who drive you crazy better than a large ship in the middle of the ocean? We have cruised two oceans, the Gulf of Mexico, and the Mediterranean and enjoyed it all. Frankly, when I get on a cruise ship I could care less where it goes, as long as it is far enough away so that I am not tempted to turn my smartphone on.

I have snorkeled and almost drowned at three different beaches. I have discovered you can order multiple menu items without fear of being ridiculed by the waiter or waitress. I have discovered the coffee bar has the best desserts I have ever tasted. I have been massaged, entertained, enlightened, and enjoyed it all without the benefit of ever setting foot on land.

I have learned Spanish, and I know where the best drugstores are throughout the Caribbean. I have rested on the prettiest white sand beaches God ever made. I even got to be Elvis and James Brown in the ship's show on the last night.

Someone once told me that everybody needs something to look forward to. I look forward to seeing sapphire blue waters and white sand. I look forward to the music of the islands and foods you can't get in the mall food court.

I have done my math, and a month on a cruise ship is actually cheaper than a month in an assisted living center. In a few years, you can contact me through Carnival Cruise lines.

Drop a note in a bottle and I'll get right back to you.

Chapter 15
You Just Work One Day a Week

I received a text message from a young member of our church. Her class assignment in high school was to "shadow" an adult she knows and observe what they do for a living. I was initially flattered that she wanted to shadow her minister for a day. Our families are close friends, and I thought it would be a blast to show her what a minister does.

Just a few days away from the big event, I became petrified. Most lay people have no idea what a minister's life and week entails. Countless numbers of wise guys have told me over the years that it must be nice to work just one day a week. I smile and try to be cordial, but it really ticks me off.

My problem is I never know what kind of day I am going to have. It is part of the charm of the ministry. The type of day I have is in direct proportion to the type of day my members are having. If they are having surgery or are in the hospital, that means I am going to the hospital. If no one is in the hospital, I avoid the place. There are sick people and needles in that place, and I prefer to avoid both as often as I can.

I have found many people think the minister goes to the hospital everyday regardless. I have known a few ministers of other faiths who saw the hospital wards as fertile fields for the harvest for their churches. They would visit every person in the hospital they could, wanting to introduce themselves and pray the sinner's prayer with them and any other poor soul who was visiting them at the time. It really got out of hand around ten years ago in the Charleston, South Carolina, area. The hospital chaplain's office required all ministers to sign an oath that they would only visit their church members in the hospital and stop bugging other folks. The chaplain's office caught a lot of flak from those who deemed themselves to be spiritually superior pastors.

How can I explain to a fourteen-year-old that some days in the ministry are boring? No one calls the office. No surgeries are scheduled. There are no funerals to plan or conduct. The sermon is in the hopper for Sunday. All is well for twenty-four short hours.

How will she know that four nights a week I am sitting in committee meetings, going to praise band practice, working with the children in our recreation programs, or counseling the seemingly happy couple who are near a divorce? How can you explain to her that there are some Sunday mornings you are up at six because you had an epiphany during the night and your sermon for the two services that morning seems to be suddenly inadequate? How can she understand those phone calls in the middle of the night when someone's life has just suffered a permanent change because of a death or a new life entering this world?

Will she understand after only a few hours that a good minister must be a writer, a public speaker, a counselor, a firefighter, a peacemaker, a plumber, a spouse, and a parent and must always wear a smile and have words of encouragement no matter how bad their life may suck at the time?

I doubt it. I'm just sitting here hoping someone has a minor "procedure" this week so I can show her the nifty parking spaces reserved for a minister at the hospital.

If only I worked more than one day a week.

Chapter 16
Ordered Not to Die

The homepage on my iPad is set to always bring up Yahoo! every time I turn my machine on. It contains a wealth of basically worthless information, which my brain analyzes, compartmentalizes, and flushes away until the next time I turn it on.

I ran across a story there not too long ago that has stuck in my mind because of its absurdity: "Town Council Votes To Outlaw Death."

Politicians are always trying to tell us the government is too involved in our everyday lives. Now it appears they want to become more involved in our deaths, as well. The story was just sitting there on my desktop waiting to be read, so I read it.

The problem stemmed from the fact that the town had one cemetery for the entire town and the cemetery was full. For years people had been dying to get in there, and now the space available was zilch.

I have known for years that some cemeteries, our national cemeteries for example, will bury people on top of each other. Whoever dies first gets the lower berth. It allows husbands and wives to be buried together and expands the capacity of the cemetery.

The interesting thing about this new town ordinance is that since it went into effect, not a single solitary soul in the town had passed away. There is actually a small fine assessed to the estate if a person passes away without the town council's permission.

I have pastored several churches with cemeteries. I have found cemeteries not only hold the remains of the dead but the church memberships of many lost sheep. Folks have often attended my churches but refused to join them because they had memberships at another church that offered free burials for all their church members. If they don't have your presence on this side, they will retain it on the other.

I had one church years ago that had more money in the cemetery fund than they did in all their other bank accounts combined. The preservation of the dead was more important than their ministry in the present.

I served a large church once that has a large cemetery surrounding it on three sides. On an average Sunday, we had nine hundred at our services, but only two hundred sixty were still breathing. The influence of the other six hundred forty was often more powerful than any words or acts of the two hundred sixty on this side of the property.

Perhaps you should consider passing a motion at your next council meeting outlawing death in your congregation if you feel your cemetery is nearing capacity and burying people on top of each other just isn't Methodist.

It's not that I dislike conducting a funeral. I'd much rather have five funerals than one wedding. We just need to jump on this "no death" trend before the Baptists do.

Chapter 17
Circus Peanuts Are Not a Health Food

For most of my adult life, I have been a larger than normal guy. I have been on every diet science and Hollywood have offered. I have enjoyed success with most of them. The success was often followed by a return to my prior clothing size.

Last week at one of our church suppers, a church member called me over and asked me a question. They asked me a low-down question: What happened to that forty pounds you lost?

I replied that thirty or so of them had returned home.

Have you ever noticed it is always the thin people who ask such questions? Nobody heavier than two hundred pounds would ask another "just my size" person such a question.

Yet it was a fair question. Last year I had spoken about the benefits of eating circus peanuts. They are an orange, peanut-shaped marshmallow treat sold in stores everywhere for people like me. I ate them by the boxcar full. They are very low in fat but contain more sugar than Cuba does.

Very intelligent scientists, dare I say geniuses, have now discovered that "just my size" people may very well be that way because of their genetic make-up. We are not just fat, overeating slobs. Our bodies have a built-in disposition to store fat in certain places and in certain amounts.

I have a copy of that article. I call it the Just My Size Magna Carta. We were created by God to be the way we are. Dieting may cause the weight to leave for a while, but like a good coon dog, it comes back at feeding time.

This means to me that I can enjoy the four major food groups (Big Mac, Fries, Shake, and Apple Pie) without hiding at the corner table at McDonald's. If I had known this when my children were young, their Easter chocolate rabbits would still have had their ears and tail.

This doesn't mean I have not had periods of success with dieting. The Atkins Diet has been a favorite of mine. You can eat all the red meat and poultry products you can hold each day. You just don't eat sugar or flour or rice or potatoes. I ate so much red meat the Chick-fil-A cows were sending me threatening messages.

After six months of this diet, I ran across a Cadbury egg someplace and I ate it, starting a complete reversal of my diet, then went back to enjoying the processed sugars God intended me to have.

Now that I again have a Broyhill figure (my chest has fallen into my drawers) I am going to rejoice that God has made me this way. I consider thin people to be folks that haven't fully developed yet. People go to bed hungry across the world every night. We should be grateful we have enough to eat.

Therefore, my spiritual advice to you is if someone offers you a fried pork chop, take it and eat it. Children may still be starving in China.

Chapter 18
I Hate Sunday Evenings

Sunday nights were an almost sacred time in my household as a child. Leftovers from lunch were combined with a cake of fresh cornbread along with sliced tomatoes and ears of corn, and my extended family would sit around the family table and enjoy fellowship and eat. It was a given that we all had attended church that morning, and we would compare notes regarding attendance and who wasn't there and would try to remember what the preacher had so strenuously preached about seven scant hours before.

As I grew older, accepted my first appointment, got married, and moved to places only Rand-McNally knew about, I found it more difficult to make those Sunday suppers. Every night, however, around eight o'clock my mother would call me and ask me her roll call of questions.

"How many did you have in church today" was always the first question she asked. She always thought the number in church was determined by how her son was doing as its pastor. I never had the heart to tell her it had more to do with the weather, the season (football or vacation), and other factors beyond the control of any pastor.

She always asked other relevant questions, such as are the grandkids still living, how's my wife, when are you coming home, etc. She would then tell me who did make it to supper and lay a little guilt on me because I could not be there. She was a perfect Wesleyan mother with Jewish tendencies.

The years went by, and soon those Sunday night suppers became cozy little suppers for four. Families expanded, and soon they had their own Sunday night suppers with their kids and grandkids.

Every Sunday night at eight, however, my mother still called me. I set my clock and my heart by those calls.

One Sunday night came and went, and the phone didn't ring. I waited a couple days and called her, and a stranger answered the phone. It was my mother's voice, but my mother had left me. While it seemed to me her dementia had struck suddenly, I realized as I recalled moments and conversations that it had not. I simply had been trying to wish it away. My mother had forgotten who I was as easily as she had forgotten the day of the week.

It's been several years now since my phone calls stopped. My mother sat beside me in a funeral chapel as the man she had been married to for seventy-three years laid in repose. She had no idea who he was.

My mother is still alive and living in a full nursing facility. I go to see her not because she knows who I am, but because I know who she is. We have short visits, and now I ask the same questions each week. I rarely get a discernible answer. I always tell her I love her and she responds in kind. Dementia has not taken away her kindness as she tells this stranger she loves him.

Now I dread Sunday nights. I hate them. It is a time of mourning the death of someone who is still living, of mourning a time in my life I didn't fully appreciate and, perhaps, a person I did not appreciate enough either.

Eight o'clock comes and goes, and another week is done.

Chapter 19
H-D Stands for Hot Dog

When I was a teenager, I was amazed at the stories my dad would tell me about my parents' adventures on his Harley-Davidson motorcycle. It was amazing to me that these two people, who seemed to want to deny me the pleasures of life I so desired, once threw a leg over a 750-pound motorcycle and rode off into the sunset. They had photographs of them together on the bike. My mother is afraid of flying and boats, but she rode on the back of a motorcycle. Amazing!

I had a trail bike when I was a young teenager but soon fell out of love with it when I got my driver's license at the ridiculously young age of fifteen. My parents sold my bike and bought me a used AMC lime green Javelin that became my preferred means of transportation for the next three years. I forgot about motorcycles.

Then something clicked in my brain when I was in my mid-forties. It happened after I had a lengthy shoulder surgery in the hospital and discovered they had drugs that could make almost any pain go away for four hours at a time. I wanted to ride a motorcycle again. I started reading about motorcycles and looking online for models that a middle-aged fat man would look good on. It became apparent I would not look right on anything other than a Harley-Davidson.

I waited until my last child was through with college, and vice versa, to start buying motorcycles. My wife shared my desire to ride, and we both bought small bikes and worked our way up to the big cruising bikes. I finally bought the bike of my dreams, a Harley-Davidson model appropriately named "Fatboy." I loved that bike, and we rode everywhere in our area together. We discovered Bike Weeks in Myrtle Beach and Daytona Beach. We rode the Blue Ridge Parkway and enjoyed the coolness of a mountain road.

If you own a Harley, you find out the bike cost $20,000 and the clothing cost you more than that. We have Harley T-shirts, dress shirts, hats, pants, jackets, caps, and sleepwear. I have a tattoo on my right shoulder that says simply H-D. It stands for Harley-Davidson, but my wife says it should stand for a "hundred dollars" because we have never left a Harley store without spending that much.

One thing I never really considered before becoming a biker was the reaction it provoked among my church people. Many of the guys were envious. They wanted to buy a bike, but their wives wouldn't let them. Some of the folks, young and older alike, wanted a ride with the pastor or his wife.

Everyone was not happy about their pastor becoming a biker. Their image of a biker was of the beer-drinking, hard-living, foul-mouthed, drug-taking scoundrel who passed them driving ninety on the interstate. The idea that their pastor would associate with such a crowd shocked the blue right out of their hair.

I found out the stereotype of a biker was wrong. In twenty years of riding, I have never seen two bikers get in a fight or leave another biker stranded on the road. All economic and social class divisions end when you hit the start button on a Harley. No matter what you do the rest of the week, you are all the same when you are riding on two wheels.

You may have noticed most bikers have a distinctive wave to each other when they pass on the highway. It's not a means of saying hello. It's a sign of the brotherhood that exists between bikers.

I saw a pamphlet a Christian motorcycle group printed once that said, "If Jesus walked on earth today, he would ride a motorcycle." I can picture in my mind Jesus and his motorcycle club of twelve riding in formation down the highway of life. He would be out front riding his Harley, probably one of those new sporty models. His hair would be flowing in the wind, and he would have the surest sign of a happy bike rider—bugs in his front teeth.

That's an image of Jesus that could preach.

Chapter 20
Giving the Church the Bird

Unlike medical school or law school, seminary does a great job of preparing a person theologically for the ministry but a poor job of teaching you how to handle the real day-to-day issues of being a pastor. The following is a true story that reminds me perhaps I should have majored in animal husbandry in college.

Just when you think you have faced every problem in a church that could possibly happen, something comes along that you have never had to handle before. My custodian recently came rushing into my office, out of breath and red-faced, with a look of concern in his eyes.

"There's a pigeon in the kitchen and I can't get it out."

I immediately put down my work, my Bible, and my Diet Coke, and together we descended into the bowels of the church to rid ourselves of this fowl creature.

When we arrived, the bird was perched comfortably on top of our stove vent, just above our freshly painted cabinets. We looked, but could not find, an outside opening from which the bird had made his way into our safe sanctuary. He was too fat to come in through the mail slot. We were completely stumped!

The immediate problem was not in figuring out how it got in but how we were going to get it out. We started out using the kinder, gentler method. Two grown men stood at a distance yelling "Shoo, bird!" at the top of our lungs. We opened the doors and windows, but the bird preferred his lofty perch to our sincere invitations to leave.

When it became obvious he wasn't leaving, we tried some not-so-gentle persuasion. The custodian went in with a mop handle and tried to drive him toward the window. Doing its imitation of a Japanese dive-bomber, the bird dove at him and sent him screeching from the kitchen before returning to his perch above the stove.

Being an old baseball pitcher, I went to my car to retrieve a baseball. If the custodian could not sweep him out, maybe I could knock him out. I stood in the kitchen for five minutes, eyeball to eyeball with my feathered adversary. If I missed and struck the cabinets, it would no doubt leave a mark.

After weighing the options afforded me, and not wanting to have an army of angry women out for my hide for marking up the cabinets, I decided having a church pet was not a bad thing after all. We tried to coax him down with food, but all we could find were stale communion wafers, which I would not have wanted.

We decided to leave him in the kitchen with the doors closed and the windows opened. We gave the bird the option of leaving our church on its own.

I know God sent his Holy Spirit down upon Jesus in the form of a dove, but I am not sure who sent this pigeon or what he wanted.

The next morning, he had flown the coop, taking a communion wafer with him. Several days later I found a dead pigeon that resembled our former guest in the church parking lot.

I hope it wasn't the wafer.

Chapter 21
I'm a Large

I received a message on Facebook informing me that my Little League baseball coach, Ed Austin, passed away. He died from leukemia, which has taken far too many people from my life. He was in his eighties and lived a life that made writing his obituary easy for his family. The obit told the true story of a man who was kind, caring, and hard working in his church and community.

I went to school for the first twelve years with his son, Rodney. When we were old enough to play baseball, his dad volunteered to coach the team. He worked eight hours in the local textile mill and came directly to the ballfield to handle fifteen eleven- and twelve-year-olds. I had never played on an organized team before. I grew up before the age of tee ball and coaches pitch. Softball at recess had been my only stab at organized baseball at that point.

One day he told the team our catcher would not be able to play that week. He asked if anyone could catch. I immediately raised my hand, even though I had never worn a catcher's mitt in my life. I put on the "tools of ignorance" and squatted behind home plate as the coach's son pitched to me. I must have done all right because no one else tried to catch. The position was mine.

After practice, the coach asked me if I had a cup. I had no idea what he meant. I found out the cup he was talking about was a very important piece of personal protection for a twelve-year-old. He told me I needed to get my mother to carry me into town and buy one before the game because I had to have one on to play.

Explaining this to my mother was the most difficult thing I ever had to do in sports. She obviously had never worn one or even heard of one. She asked me if that was something I put in my glove so I could catch the ball better. I told her she was close, but I thought she had it backwards.

She carried me into town to Crutchfield's sporting goods store. We went in, and I suddenly became very shy about asking the salesman for what I came for. He was an old acquaintance of our family. He had once played ball for my father when he was a young man. It was my mother who told him what I needed, and he got a big smile on his face.

He looked at me and asked me, "Son, what size do you wear?"

Size? I didn't know those things came in sizes. I proudly stuck out my chest and said, "Large!"

After an awkward pause, he said, "No, son, I mean your pant size. It comes in a strap with a holder that fits around your waist."

For the last time in my life, I was able to say I wear a medium.

I got my cup and athletic supporter and proudly caught for my teams for the next eight years. I found Coach Austin was right—it was a handy piece of equipment to have on.

They say God works in mysterious ways. The salesman at the store was Elmer Mason. I married his daughter some eleven years after this business exchange. I don't know if he ever recalled our meeting, but I never forgot it.

Both of our sons went on to become catchers at one point in their baseball careers. Now that we can only be an athletic supporter ourselves, we can finally throw away the old bags of equipment we have saved and moved numerous times.

Yet every time I hear someone say, "I am a large," I have a slight smile upon my face for reasons known only unto me.

Chapter 22
I Stand Corrected

Once upon a time I opined about the folly of old men spending their retirement years walking dogs at 11 p.m. I openly mocked such behavior and said that was not how I was going to spend my retirement years.

I felt very safe in saying that because we were cat owners. We spent thirty years being caretakers and slaves to two different cats. They were far less trouble than caring for a dog. One was an inside-outside cat who was a marvelous pet. My wife had raised him from three days old, and he actually acted more like a cat than a dog.

Just two weeks after his death, one of the church youths showed up at our doorstep with a young kitten they found behind the church. She soon was named Cricket and spent her fifteen years on this earth as an inside cat in several different parsonages. That cat had two distinctive positive traits: she loved me, and she loved to chase our friend Scott around the house on her back legs when he and his wife, Allison, came to visit.

The day we put her down at the vet's office was the last day I ever thought we would have a pet. We both cried out loud when they took her away. The cat actually stretched her paw through her carrier and patted my wife on her hand as if to say it was going to be all right.

On the way home, we both agreed we would not have another pet. We were adamant about that. We couldn't go through that again.

Fast forward five years. We were comfortably retired near North Myrtle Beach. Our days were ours to spend any way we wanted to. Our biggest summertime decision was whether to go to the beach or up the street to the community pool.

Then my wife received a phone message, from our neighbors who have several dogs, that the breeder they got their Goldendoodle from had puppies for sale. My wife said call the breeder and see if we can just go by and look at the puppies. It was the same day the boys from Langley shot down the Chinese balloon as we watched from the beach.

That's the same line I told my wife when I said, "Let's just go look at the new cars and see what they look like." It was the same line I said many times about going to The Guitar Center to buy strings and came out with a new guitar, or three.

I knew I was in deep trouble.

When we arrived, my wife immediately went to a pretty little white puppy and held it up to her cheek. I knew I was suddenly a poorer man. I paid a down payment on a female puppy named Layla. Two weeks later, I went back with a bag of cash and bought our first puppy. She cost more than our first new car. I know, it was a 1979 Pinto, but the principle still applies.

Our lives changed immediately. God did bless us with a puppy who slept all night, but I had never housebroken anything in my life, including our sons, Matt and Jon. My wife spent those two weeks reading everything she could about Goldendoodles. We bought a kennel and enough dog treats for the entire local humane society. It took a week or so, but I got used to walking that little puppy and became an expert poopie scooper.

Life had a new normal.

Then we got a second phone call. They had two more puppies. I made a low-ball offer for one after my wife asked, "Do we really need another puppy?" Probably not, but I didn't need nine guitars either. A neighbor donated another kennel to the cause, and I spent another sum of money to bring her home.

I named her Ginger after some deep thought on the matter. It came down to Ruby or Ginger because she was a deep rusty color. I was going to go with Ruby, which was my mother's name, until I thought about standing out in the dark at 10:30 at night and telling a dog, "Ruby, would you hurry up and do your do." It just didn't seem right.

So, we now have two Goldendoodles who weigh sixty-five pounds each. I have an app on my phone that tracks my steps and movements (i.e., the same app that got Murdaugh convicted), and I now walk around seventy miles a month, mostly to the dog area and back.

I am doing more than the guys I laughed at fifteen years before.

Have you ever noticed God is always listening? The very things I have ridiculed in life, including people and events, I've had to face myself. It's like God thought, "That would be a great teaching moment."

Two weeks after getting the second dog, my wife remarked that two are a lot of work.

I told her I could sell Ginger and make some money.

Her reply was, "You are NOT selling MY dog."

Now I'm the walking and scooping champion of Longs, South Carolina. You can find me outstanding in my field.

Chapter 23
Stoned on a Cruise Ship

Every morning when I wake up, I do an inventory of working and non-working parts. Sometimes it's a knee or a hip. Sometimes my back is stiff, and I do the zombie walk toward the bathroom hoping that somewhere between the bed and the toilet my gait will return to that of a normal person.

I've had back troubles for decades. The doctor told me my back was too straight. It sure didn't feel too straight. I started going to see a chiropractor who jerked and popped me until I popped like an old rocking chair in the wind.

Some years ago, my wife and I were on a cruise of the west coast of Mexico. We were enjoying the beautiful sights of Cabo San Lucas when I started having what I thought were back spasms. They got worse as the afternoon went on, and I decided to seek a local medicine doctor to help me. I found a local La Pharmacia and gingerly went in seeking help from what felt like a knife in the kidney.

The pharmacist did not speak English. "No hablo Ingles," he told me.

"I no hablo Espanol," I replied.

That was my first mistake. Using sign language and very broken Spanish, he got the message my back hurt. I pointed to my back and made a grimace, and he seemed to understand.

The local pharmacist smiled and said, "Uno momento, senor, uno momento."

A few minutes later he returned with a ten-pack of large, white pills.

He said, "Aqui, señor, esta ayuda."

I took a chance and took two, using the male concept that if one helps, two would really help.

I was right. I had no pain and an hour later no consciousness. I went to sleep face down on the formal dinner table at dinner. Those who didn't know me thought I had been having a bottle of wine or four. Those who did know me thought I was just really tired.

I felt better the next morning and didn't take another of those pills. I got back to South Carolina, turned my iPad on, and googled those pills. He had given me a horse tranquilizer! The pill had been outlawed in the United States because their regular use caused heart damage. I had no pain, but I did have a craving for apples and carrots that lasted a week or so.

I found out later that what I was having was a kidney stone trying to leave my body. The stones were wider than the ureters God gave me when I was born. If I was a car, a recall would have been made for me a long time ago.

I have endured countless stones in the last fifteen years since that Mexican experience. My urologist also happens to be a lawyer. He can sue himself for malpractice. That precious man gave me a prescription that has kept them away for three years. Until, that is, I left the country for another cruise, leaving this time from Italy. I had not one but two stones that clawed their way out of my body in three hours' time. I'm pretty sure our next-door neighbors on either side of us were confused by the sounds coming from Room 1420. It was just a man with an incredibly small set of ureters and incredibly big kidney stones.

I have heard many friends and church members share with me questions they have for God when they get to heaven. I have one or two myself, and they are nearly as complex. I don't care how he made the world or why he chose me to be one of his servants and pastors.

However, I think he may have made me on a Monday, and I have to know.

Chapter 24
Till Death Us Do Part (Maybe)

I have often shared in a sermon stories about weddings I have conducted. Some of the stories are just too good not to share. I often tell people I would rather perform ten funerals to one wedding. Everything can go wrong in a wedding. The worst thing that can happen has already happened, or you would not be having a funeral. There are no mothers of the bride at a funeral, either.

I have married people on the banks of rivers, high on a mountaintop, in their homes, in gardens, on the beach, and in countless other places and churches. I have witnessed firsthand the good, the bad, and the ugly. I have experienced the bride walking out angry during a rehearsal. I have also had other brides come back years later and tell me they wished they had walked out during their wedding rehearsal.

I had a wedding a few years ago that was unique. A middle-aged couple wanted to get married on their houseboat. He was near forty, and she was thirty-one. Neither had ever been married. They invited the entire clan down from the hills of North Carolina, and forty of us set sail on a sixty-eight-foot houseboat.

As we were getting in place for the ceremony, a bass boat came screaming up behind our boat with four invitees who had literally missed the boat at the dock. Sailboaters and fishermen alike pulled their boats up close to the houseboat to watch the ceremony and cheer the couple on. They all sounded their horns when the couple said "I do" and sealed it with a kiss.

What made this wedding unique was that the groom was an injured veteran who was now restricted to a wheelchair. Determined to walk down the aisle, he worked for months to build up enough strength to put on his leg braces and struggle down the aisle with his new wife. There wasn't a dry eye, or seat, on the boat by the time the ceremony was over.

Unfortunately for them, they got a glimpse very quickly of what married life sometimes is like. When they returned to the dock, someone plugged their power supply into the wrong receptacle, and their television burned up as guests prepared to abandon ship. The caterer failed to show up. Two friends of the bride took several bags of chips and a wedding cake and did what Jesus did with the loaves and fishes.

I found out sometime later that the beer and wine eventually showed up and the groom got smashed as the night went on. His wife became disgusted by his behavior and dumped him in the lake, wheelchair and all. The best man and two others had to go into the water to retrieve him and the chair. On their way back home the next day, they stopped at a rest area. When they went back to their car, it was gone.

I understand this couple is still married and still boating. I guess they found a way to keep their marriage, and their boat, afloat.

One of the last weddings I performed involved a young lady who was five when I left her church. She asked me to please officiate her wedding, so I agreed.

I had never met her groom. I didn't even know his name. I asked for the wedding license prior to the wedding so I could finish the paperwork and learn what his name was. I thought I was smart … I was wrong.

During the vows, I called him by the wrong name. Twice. His bride corrected me, and I apologized and she said just get on with the service. Those attending laughed out loud. The mother of the groom almost fell out of her chair, doubled over from laughing at my faux pas.

Did I mention I dislike weddings?

Chapter 25
The Snow We Didn't Get

Author's note: There is nothing that excites those of us raised in the South more than a few inches of snow and a snow day. A snowfall that would be laughed away in Cleveland paralyzes the South.

When we moved to the Lowcountry of South Carolina, we told our children they would not see snow again until we moved back to the Upstate. It snowed twice the first year we were in the Lowcountry. The two snows together may have registered two inches. There is nothing like taking a picture of a palmetto tree covered in snow with frozen Spanish moss hanging from it.

A couple of years ago, we had winter storm warnings for Myrtle Beach three weekends in a row. They used ten years' worth of salt and sand on the bridges in that one month.

The following was written when we lived Upstate and our children were in school. It speaks to the greatest disappointment in a Southern school child's life: a blown weather forecast for snow. Meteorologists are the only people I know who can be right half the time and keep their jobs. This is for anybody who ever got their sled out for no reason.

I hope all of you enjoyed the three inches of snow we got Sunday night and Monday morning as much as we did. We woke up in the middle of the night hoping to see the yards covered in white, only to be disappointed. The weather man was wrong again!

Schoolchildren across the Upstate have erupted in anger. One teacher at Walhalla Primary School has allowed her class to write a letter to the local television weatherman in protest of their failed prophesy.

Snow is special to us in the South. Plants and schools close down when just a few inches of the white stuff fall to earth. The sleds are brought out of hiding, and the vanilla flavoring is discovered in the back of the pantry shelf in anticipation of a morning of sledding and snow cream.

Maybe it wasn't the weatherman's fault. He has satellites and various radar units that can spot dewfall at forty miles. Snow is a little trickier to predict down here.

Maybe he should buy himself a weather rock. You place the rock outside your window and look at it every morning. If the rock is shiny, the sun is out. If it is wet, it's raining. If it is white, it snowed last night. If it is gone, it could be a touch windy today.

After it was apparent it wasn't snowing and everyone was going to school and work on time, they ran a weather update. The chances of snow went away when the weatherman noticed the sun was out and not a cloud was in the sky.

In the Old Testament days, such a failed prophecy would have been met with a violent reaction. False prophets were taken outside the city wall and stoned to death. They were never wrong twice.

The local meteorologists can rest easy tonight. There is no city wall we can take them to for stoning. I just want them to realize tonight when they go to bed that they broke the hearts of thousands of little children, and many childish adults like me.

Maybe they will buy themselves a weather rock. They need one really bad.

Chapter 26
I've Got a Monkey on My Back

Addiction is a word that we, unfortunately, hear too much in our world today. The prisons are full of people who became addicted to illegal and prescription drugs and turned to crime to get their daily fix. There is no minister who has served for any length of time who has not been asked to try to help an alcoholic church member or a family member of an alcoholic. Alcoholics Anonymous groups meet in thousands of churches, trying to change the lifestyle and habits of those whose lives have been wrecked by alcohol.

The greatest addiction problem remains nicotine. Both of my sons still smoke, even though they watched their grandfather succumb to lung cancer as children. I smoked a pipe when I was in seminary because I thought it made me look more scholarly. I needed all the help I could get in that area. I gave up smoking a pipe when my oldest son went through the house as a toddler holding my pipe in his hand.

While I am not addicted to drugs, alcohol, or nicotine, I still have a huge monkey on my back. I am addicted to Diet Coke. I go into withdrawals if I know we are out of that artificially sweetened nectar of the gods. My wife once bought me a dorm room sized refrigerator to put in my office so I could always have a chilled stash within arm's reach.

My addiction started while I was still in seminary. In an attempt to lose weight, I stopped drinking regular Coke and started drinking Tab. Tab tasted like bug spray smells. I never worried about being addicted to Tab.

The Coca-Cola corporation soon came out with this new drink called Diet Coke. It was supposed to taste like regular Coke. I beat a path to the student center and bought my first Diet Coke. Smokers remember their first cigarette. Drinkers remember their first beer. I remember that first Diet Coke.

It went down sweet and smooth, and I could not wait to buy a six pack and head home.

Since that time, I have added it up and I have drunk somewhere in the neighborhood of 82,340 Diet Cokes. The number would be much higher if it wasn't for the two times I thought I had kicked my habit.

I went six months without a Diet Coke once. Thank God the Charleston Police Department was able to talk me down off the Ravenel Bridge. I did not want to live knowing bottled water and iced tea were going to be my only beverages for the rest of my life.

I now, without remorse, keep Diet Coke stashed at my office and home. It must be Diet Coke. Not Diet Pepsi, not Diet Orange or Grape, not unsweetened tea. It ticks me off when I order Diet Coke in a restaurant and the waiter or waitress says, "Is Diet Pepsi all right?" NO, IT'S NOT ALL RIGHT. They act as if the two are interchangeable. They are not. Morons!

Now medical science is trying to rain on my parade. They are telling me that drinking diet drinks makes you put on weight. I remember the first time I heard that I put down my Diet Coke and Snickers bar and fired off an email in response to such blasphemy. The absurd claim is that the artificial sweetener causes your brain to want to eat more sweet foods that are not artificially sweetened. It's hard to believe they spent millions of our taxpayers' dollars studying this subject and that was the best they could come up with?

Our scientists also said that if you force-fed laboratory rats five gallons of Diet Coke a day for ten years, they would develop bladder cancer. Bladder cancer is nothing to play with. I bet catheterizing those poor rats was not much fun.

I have a Diet Coke with my bacon, eggs, and cheese every morning, and nothing bad has happened to me. Every man my age has heart palpitations, high blood pressure, and high cholesterol. It is a Southern heritage and right.

A couple of years ago, Coca-Cola came out with a new diet drink called Coke Zero. This drink is based on the "new" Coke that fell flat on its face two decades ago. It has zero calories, zero fat, zero carbs, and zero protein. I drink one occasionally, but every time I do I feel like I am cheating on my one true love.

Sorry, got to run. Got a cold one in the fridge calling my name.

Chapter 27
Adios Summer

Author's note: There is a phenomenon in the church that happens every year. It's called summer. Each summer, attendance drops, giving slows to a crawl, and pastors take well-earned vacations. This is a story I wrote regarding the "summer slump."

If Labor Day is the official end of summer, it cannot come too soon for me again this year. As a person built for comfort instead of speed (i.e., fat), summertime is uncomfortable for me. I don't like sticking to my clothes, my car seats, my office chair, and even the pulpit chair each Sunday. I am tired of humidity and muggy nights when the air conditioner is trying its best to keep you cool by running overtime. Only the power company enjoys that process.

I also don't like cutting grass. Having a push lawnmower was a major reason my wife and I decided to have children. Like the scene from *The Godfather*, I prayed for a masculine child each time so I could train them both to be our personal gardeners. After watching them try to run over each other with the lawnmower one Saturday, I decided for the longevity of the family tree, I should cut the grass myself. I found out years later that had been their plan all along.

March 15 and October 15 became the official lawn mowing season at our house. I did not care how tall the weeds got before March 15. They were safe until then. After October 15, I prayed for a killer frost each year.

I know few ministers who enjoy summer. Our people go on vacations all over the world that often last from one to three weeks. Attendance drops in the summertime, and that means the finances suffer as well. The minister and the church treasurer look forward to Labor Day for many of the same reasons each year.

When we lived near Myrtle Beach, we circled Labor Day on the calendar each year. Half the state of Ohio relocated to the Grand Strand each summer. They were not the best of drivers, nor were they the most hospitable of folks. We used to sit beside the road and wave goodbye each Labor Day to them as they caravanned back to Ohio. To this day, next to Ann Arbor, there are more Michigan fans in Myrtle Beach than anywhere else in America.

Labor Day means all the schools are finally back in session. Other than the occasional driver's education car, the streets are safer and less congested. Folks venture out again after having been holed up for the last three months. Life is good again.

So I say a fond farewell to summer. I welcome back all my church members who have baked themselves to a toasty brown at the beaches, lakes, and mountains. I can take the church treasurer off suicide watch for another nine months, and we can get the electricity turned back on at church.

So goodbye summer. You gave us your best shot, and we survived again. Don't call us, we'll call you.

Chapter 28
December 9, 1995

There are certain dates we have in our lives when we can say with all confidence that life changed that day. For the greatest generation, which my parents were part of, December 7, 1941, would never be forgotten. After we entered the war, my father was drafted in 1943, and he left New Orleans for England. My mother did not see him until mid-1946.

Today's generation will remember September 11, 2001. Our lives became complicated after that terrible day. We lost our sense of security as a nation and as individuals. Thousands of young men and women volunteered to serve our country in foreign places that did not resemble home at all.

For our family, December 9, 1995, was a date that changed many things. My wife and I were helping Santa by doing a little shopping in a mall in Greenville, South Carolina, when we got a phone call on our bag phone. If you don't know what a bag phone is, it was a suitcase-sized phone folks carried around as a sign of being a proud member of the middle class.

Our son Matt called his mother and told her our house was on fire. My wife scolded him loudly and said, "That's not funny. Don't ever do that again," and hung up on him. We both shook our heads at the antics of a teenager.

One minute later he called back. "Why did you hang up on me?" he asked. This time we heard fire trucks and sirens in the background. The house was on fire.

We sprinted to our car and made the fastest trip we ever made from the mall to our house off Augusta Road. We were in shock. The entire neighborhood was across the street watching our lives burn. Our neighborhood consisted of the newly wed and the nearly dead, and they all were there.

We found both of our sons and were greatly relieved.

This would be a great time to say my wife and sons are scared to death of spiders. I hate snakes. We had a deal that I would kill spiders, and they would kill any snakes that slithered by.

Our youngest son, Jon, had poured camping fuel on a huge spider nest in the basement and lit it on fire to kill all those devilish creatures. He thought he had put the fire out, but a spark fell onto the carpet the church had stored in the basement. Ten minutes later all the smoke alarms went off.

The first thing I did was take my youngest son into our car. I told my child I didn't care about the house or anything that was in it. All I cared about was knowing he and his brother were safe.

I left him in the car and walked past the firemen in the house as it burned. I went to the refrigerator and got a Diet Coke out and went outside and sat on my front steps. I called my oldest son over, and he sat beside me.

As the neighbors were being entertained by our situation, I told my son the sagest words I've ever shared with him.

I said, "Matt, don't ever let them see you sweat."

We sat together on our house steps as the things we thought we held so dear literally went up in smoke.

The chairman of our trustees, who I'd talked into taking the job because it wouldn't take much time, came and stood with my wife and me on the front lawn.

My wife suddenly got a worried look. I asked what's wrong.

She said, "The firemen are going to see our Frederick's of Hollywood catalog in our bedroom." Horror of horrors!

The chairman's wife leaned over and told us, "Don't worry. If yours burns, I can give you ours."

People watching had to wonder why I was bent over laughing while our life's belongings were lost.

That was a day where we learned that things are temporary. Very temporary. When your life is on fire is a good time to take inventory of what really matters in life. When your life is on fire, you learn who you can trust and who you can't. You have a deeper appreciation for those who walk through the flames with you.

And those who laugh through the troubles with you are priceless.

Chapter 29
I'm Waiting for Jesus and I'm Ready To Go

As I have pontificated before, my family has lived in a bunch of different places. We spent the first night in thirteen different new places. In each place, my wife has done a marvelous job in trying to turn a strange house into our home.

Yet there is a feeling that creeps into my heart on occasion that reminds me that where I am is not home. Being separated from our family by distance, holidays we used to spend together are now opportunities for that feeling of homesickness to enter in. I have attempted to placate those feelings over the years by reminding myself that where I grew up and went to high school is my real home. My parents lived there all their lives, and my extended family still lives there. I have just been working out of town for the last forty-four years, waiting for the day I get to move back home.

I know that is a fallacy now. Home is not "home" anymore. My parents have relocated to heaven, the small towns have grown, and many of my class-mates have passed away, moved away, or been sent away for indefinite stays courtesy of the state. The place I wanted to return home to isn't there and may have never been there at all. The image I had of "home" was more fiction than fact. I know now I will not retire there nor live out my last days there because "home" has changed. It has betrayed me. It refused to stay the same.

I am beginning to understand more and more each day that the place I long to return to is not of this world. We all have images of what heaven will be like. What it actually is remains somewhat of a mystery. I know who rules there and many of its residents. While I didn't own a home of my own until a few years ago, I know there is one being built for me there. I envision it having a view of the ocean from the front porch and a view of the Appalachian Mountains from the back porch.

What it actually shall be, though, is not as important as having a place to go to in that zip code when you die.

I believe the Lord gives us little glimpses of heaven while we are still here. I recently traveled two hundred miles to see our children and grandchildren. When he saw me, my grandson jumped up and came over and hugged me. If heaven is better than that, I can't imagine it.

When the family comes together after having driven miles from diverse directions just to share a meal together, that is a short glimpse of what heaven will be like.

I remind myself now when I feel homesick that one day I won't be homesick anymore. My traveling days will be over, and the movers will never come for my stuff again. I will be in the land of hellos, not goodbyes.

I wrote these verses couple of years ago:

> Hand in hand we will walk together
> On them old streets of gold.
> We will live and laugh forever
> And never grow old.
> We will be made brand new
> From our heads down to our toes.
> I'm waiting for Jesus
> And I'm ready to go.

I'll see you there, back home, soon.

Chapter 30
It's a Dog's World

My wife and I had the sad task of carrying our family dog to the vet where he was euthanized. He was around fifteen years old and had developed cancer. It was a very sad time for us both, and I am sure the dog, named Sarge by our children, was not thrilled by it either.

Sarge was a gift from God to us. On our way home from church one Sunday, we saw a Golden Retriever puppy playing in the road. We spoke about the dog's safety, and I said I had always wanted a Golden Retriever. Nothing more was thought or said about the puppy. We lived about a mile and half off the highway from the spot where we saw the dog.

The next morning, as we were trying to get out the door to go to work and school, we heard a scratching at our door. It was the puppy! I asked my wife in my best five-year-old's voice if I could keep it. She agreed to keep it just long enough for its owner to claim him. No one came forth, and for fifteen years he was ours and we were his.

Sarge lived in several church parsonages with us. He also lived with my father twice over the years. While a parsonage is supposed to be the minister's home, there are guidelines for pets. We have followed several ministers who did not follow those guidelines. We moved into one house where the previous minister had a large dog inside his house. He had positioned his recliner next to a window where he had built a shed outside opening into the window. He kept his dog and his firewood in the shed, both within arm's reach without having to go outside. His dog had literally chewed the inside shutters down to the hinges as he passed from the inside world to the outside world.

We had to leave Sarge with my dad the last four years of his life because we did not have an area to keep him. The neighborhood we lived in was inhabited by old men and small dogs. Each night when we came in, the streets were littered with both. Old men were spending their retirement walking little dogs and carrying plastic Walmart bags so that the entire outside world would not be their pet's bathroom. That is not how I plan to spend my retirement.

Having a pet is expensive now. Vets pounce on those of us with soft hearts and mediocre checking accounts each time we darken their door. A lady I know carried her pet five hundred miles to a vet for a colonoscopy. The hard part was getting the cat to drink all of that prep stuff.

Pets are like our children. However, you do not have to send them to college, bail them out of jail, move them into your basement, or soothe their broken hearts. As long as the feeder is full and the litter box is empty, you have a friend for life.

This was the third dog I had to take to the vet to be put down. My first was on Christmas Day 1978. He was dying of renal failure, and we spent Christmas Eve night at the vet's office waiting for the bad news. It wasn't a very merry Christmas for us.

Someone asked me once if I thought there would be dogs and cats in heaven. I think there will be. Most of the pets who have lived with us over the years have been nicer than most people we have dealt with who were sure they were going there when they passed on. Heaven would not be heaven without them.

I remember telling my mother when I was in grade school that I wished I were a dog. When asked why, I said, "They don't have to work or go to school, they lie around in the sun all day, and they eat and drink whenever they want."

What I was wishing for sounds like a great retirement plan. I was just sixty years ahead of myself.

It's a dog's world. Bow wow to you and yours.

Chapter 31
It's Nap Time

I was visiting a church member in the pre-op department of the hospital when their anesthesiologist came in the room. He explained to my parishioner what he was going to do. He ended by saying these words: I'm just going to help you take a little nap.

Not passing up a chance to make a smart remark, I told him we were in the same business. He said, "Oh, are you an anesthesiologist?" I said no, I'm a minister, but we both put people to sleep for a living. He did not see the humor in this but my parishioner did, which is all that mattered to me anyway.

It is not unusual for people to take a quick cat nap in church. I had one man who would have dozed if Jesus himself was preaching. He was taking a nap one Sunday in the choir loft when he dropped his book, and it made a loud bang on that hardwood floor and everyone within ten rows jumped in unison. It was the first time the church had been moved in years.

He always apologized and said it was a medical condition. When I asked him what his disease was, he said he was sick of my preaching. I don't think I was the first or last preacher he pulled that one on.

As I have become older, I have been moved by the power of a well-timed nap. There are good naps and there are bad naps. Years ago I asked the Methodist minister three towns over to come and preach our revival. He was awful. Boring. Terrible. I was sitting in the pulpit area with him and leaned my head back on the organ. I woke up somewhere between his third point and poem. Fortunately, everyone else had become comatose as well and did not notice their minister napping.

That's a bad nap.

I read a book some time back about the life of Bob Hope. He lived to be a hundred years old. Someone asked him when he was ninety-five what the secret of his longevity was, and he told them he took several power naps a day. For Bob, a power nap was ten minutes. He said he always awoke fresh and ready to continue the day.

I remember my mother, after a three-hundred-mile trip and working half a day, going to sleep standing up against her sister's refrigerator. If you can sleep and hold up a fridge, that's a power nap.

Jesus was continually trying to escape from the crowds so he could take a power nap. If it was good enough for him, why should we be embarrassed if we have to take a short siesta during the day?

I have found that my naptime keeps getting later in the day. My best nap time is my pre-bedtime nap. It's 7:30 p.m., your stomach is full, the wife has her head in her computer, the cat has settled down, and you are watching *The Wheel of Fortune*. If that isn't conducive to a nap, I don't know what is. I'll sleep for an hour or so and wake up to that "look" wives give their husbands when they have been snoring. With any luck at all, I can brush my teeth, turn the bed back, and go back to sleep.

When I was younger, the conditions had to be just right for me to go to sleep. It had to be dark, cool, a fan running, and the TV on to drone me to sleep. Not anymore. The only requirement I have to be ready for a nap is to be fully awake from the last one.

I told someone the other day that my heart tells me I am twenty-five, my head tells me I am sixty-five, and my body tells me I am seventy-five. That makes me one hundred and sixty-five years old. No wonder I need a nap.

Airplanes used to have smoking and nonsmoking sections. Maybe our churches need napping and non-napping sections. We could substitute Red Bull for grape juice and have communion every Sunday.

Just a thought.

Chapter 32
Searching for Lost Things

Author's note: As I have become older (not old) I have discovered my memory is a fickle thing. My wife and I recently were talking about kids from my first church. I could remember almost all their names. But I can't remember things like where I left my phone, glasses, keys, etc. Maybe you can relate. The following I wrote on a day when my memory failed me. I was much younger then, so age can't be a reason why it fails me now!

Tuesday got off to an awful start for me this week. As I started out the door to take my son to school, I could not find my house keys. Panic set in immediately. I have so many keys I have to use two key rings to accommodate them all. One key ring holds the car keys. The other holds my house keys, church keys, and a van key.

Life came to a screeching halt. I realized I could not lock my house, open the church doors, or get into my office. A frantic search took place. My son and I looked everywhere. We looked in all the obvious places. A search of the sofa seat cushions resulted in a find of fifty-five cents for my son. I found two candy bar wrappers, last Sunday's sports page, a pair of dirty white socks, and a baseball bat for all my efforts.

I searched high and low, but where my keys were, I did not know. (Pardon me, Dr. Seuss.) I finally gave up, left the back door unlocked, and dashed off to join the other parents in line at the school.

On the way back home, I was reminded of the story in the Bible of the woman who searched her little house from top to bottom for the coin she had lost. She did not have any coins to lose. While the coin was not worth much to others, it was worth everything to her.

She searched and searched until she found the coin. She rejoiced over her find with all her heart.

When I returned home, my search started over again in earnest. I know it would make sense to always leave your keys in the same place, but that would require starting another habit, and I have too many habits in my life now.

After an all-inclusive search, I found my keys in one of my black dress shoes. I have no idea how they got there, but as I picked up the shoe to toss it aside in anger, I heard a jingle, and a man's shoe should never jingle. My keys were found, and I rejoiced by breaking the seal on a cold Diet Coke.

The next time you think you are small or insignificant, remember how hard and how long God searched for you. There is rejoicing where he lives also when you are no longer lost but found.

No matter how lost you may consider yourself, you are never too lost for God to find you.

Chapter 33
Strike Two

Author's note: Back before the days of reality television, families throughout the South entertained themselves each warm summer evening by watching the Atlanta Braves play baseball each night. Skip Caray, Pete Van Wieren, Ernie Johnson, and Don Sutton were the four announcers paid by the Braves to describe what we were watching on the screen. They became part of our entertainment family. Sadly, time has passed, and those four are now gone.

In 1994, an event of biblical proportions shook the South and the entire baseball loving world: The Major Leagues went on strike. No evening games, no playoffs, no World Series. The result of this strike, which ended the season, was a rise in both divorces and the birth rate across the South. Players who had been our heroes were now having their names taken in vain by gray-haired Bible-toting women across the land.

I wrote the following in April 1995 when the strike was over. I hope it brings back happy memories.

An event happened at the Strong house Sunday afternoon that I thought might never happen again: As a family, we sat down together and watched the real Atlanta Braves play baseball on television.

Perhaps you remember my sadness last year when the boys of summer went out on strike. There was more sadness at our house than there was in Mudville when the mighty Casey went down swinging. My evening entertainment had disappeared.

What we did not know last August was how long the baseball strike would last. They did not play the World Series, for goodness sake! We had to watch regular programming at night, which gave me plenty of sermon ideas but little entertainment.

The players had to start playing baseball again. The war of words had turned downright ugly. The players were being called lazy, shiftless, greedy, and hardheaded—and that was just by their wives! One player was losing $40,000 a game because of the strike. Don't you know his wife was glad to see him leave the house and start playing baseball again.

My wife has expressed the same sentiment much of the public has expressed and continues to express. She said she didn't want to watch those players play anymore. She said it's not the same since they went out on strike.

That's true. But it isn't half bad, either. There are just so many times a person can watch *Rescue 911* before they start pulling against the victims. *Northern Exposure* leaves me cold. I can only watch five minutes of *60 Minutes*. *Picket Fences* often slips through my viewing cracks. There is no hope for *Chicago Hope*. And I have watched so much of the O.J. Simpson trial I am now convinced Judge Ito did it!

So give me baseball. I think it is ironic that my first televised Braves game was on Easter Sunday. My spring spirit can truly be revived.

Welcome back Skip, Pete, Don, and Ernie. Please never leave us again.

Chapter 34
Root Canals, Kidney Stones, Hospital Visits, and Other Painful Things

When I was appointed to my first charge, I was twenty-two years old. Bishop Tullis sent me to follow a sixty-five-year-old soon-to-be-retiree who had forgotten more about the ministry than I knew at that time. He and his wife were very gracious to me during the change. I realize now they were only days away from the promised land of retirement and were just happy with life.

I knew going in the two things I disliked more than anything in life were going to the funeral home and going to the hospital. My mother would carry me to the funeral home with her when she was paying her respects to someone, and I would ask to stay in the car. I soon found out the only thing creepier than going inside the funeral home was sitting by yourself in the parking lot of a funeral home at night.

As a new student pastor, I was required to go to Local Pastor's School. It was a two-week training event the church would have so they would not just throw us out there on our own. Chaplain Talmage Skinner was one of the instructors, and he talked about how to make a correct hospital visit. He told us all to go and buy clergy collar shirts so the nurses and staff would recognize that we were ministers. He also said never let someone in a white coat tell you that you can't see your church member.

I bought four, and that started a tradition that lasted for forty years.

What he did not train us for were those occasions when a hospital visit went sideways. I had several that went that way over forty-plus years of visiting.

I pastored a church in Greenville, South Carolina, that was only five minutes from the hospital. My secretary came to my door and said, "You have an urgent call from a church member from the hospital."

I immediately took the call.

The lady was beside herself. "He's gone, He's gone," she said between the soulful sobs.

I asked, "Who's gone?"

"My husband is gone!"

I thought he had died. She certainly gave me no reason to think otherwise.

I left my office in a rush and made the five-minute trip to the hospital. It took me no longer than ten minutes to get from the cozy confines of my office to the man's hospital room.

I prayed quietly going up in the elevator that God would give me the right words to say to the grieving widow. These were opportunities to help someone that they never forget. Don't blow it, I thought.

I took a deep breath and walked into the room. He was sitting up in bed drinking orange juice. His wife and two sisters were sitting around his bed having a happy conversation.

A nurse came up to me with a Mona Lisa smile and whispered in my ear, "Come by the nurse's station when you leave, and we will tell you what happened."

I had a very strange five-minute visit and left with a quick prayer. When I got to the nurse's station, they were all rolling on the desk laughing.

The nurse who spoke to me came up. "You are not going to believe this. We were having trouble finding a vein to change his IV. Two of us tried both his arms, and we could not get a vein to cooperate. I turned to the medical technologist and said, 'I guess we can see if we can start one in his groin.' He thought we were going to stick him in his, well, you know, his doohickey, and he fainted in the bed."

I laughed out loud and then I thought, "I'd probably have fainted, too."

The man did die some months later. I was asked to preach at his funeral, and it took all my willpower not to share that story. From that moment on, whenever they came in to start or change an IV with someone I was visiting, I sprinted it to the parking lot.

The second visit that changed my hospital visitation routine was with a sweet, eighty-six-year-old saint of the church. She was having a procedure done, and I followed up with her that afternoon.

I knocked on the door, and I heard her sweet, kind voice say, "Come in."

I walked in with a smile in my voice that changed quickly.

She was naked sitting on a bedpan doing what you do on a bedpan. Without embarrassment she looked at me and said, "Preacher, just the person I wanted to see. I need to talk to you about something."

As I moonwalked backwards out of the room, I said in my best Arnold Schwarzenegger voice, "I'll be back." The next time I saw her was in church!

I have learned to ask a nurse if I can see a patient if the door is closed. There are some things that cannot be unseen, nor forgotten, and no clerical collar can undo those things.

Chapter 35
Texting for Jesus

Communications within the church have surely changed since I entered the pastorate in 1979. The small churches I pastored were in a textile mill village in upper Greenville County in South Carolina. If we wanted to know something, or if we needed to get the word out to everyone in a short period of time, we would go to the post office and tell our local postmaster. She knew everyone and had been blessed by God with an unquenchable thirst for gossip. We had telephone, telegraph, and Go and Tell Mary.

My, how things have changed! Every church with a progressive soul in it now has its own website and Facebook page. Church email lists are used to communicate everything from a death in the church family to the menu for the Wednesday night dinner. The revenue of the postal service has greatly diminished in the last ten years as email has replaced what we lovingly call snail mail.

I have a "smart" phone that delivers emails messages to me wherever I am. Personally, I always thought if the phone was really a smart phone, it would call out to me whenever I left it somewhere and couldn't find it.

Not only has the mail service taken a hit, the number of phone calls made to and from the pastor has declined since we all learned to text. Texting is sometimes much more effective than a phone call or a face-to-face conversation. For one thing, it makes the conversation much shorter. You can put your thoughts into a sentence or two and fire them off in a text without having to pretend to listen to what the other person is trying to say. It is so annoying having to wait for the other person to shut up so you can say something intelligent.

I must admit, the autocorrect feature on my phone has caused me to send out a text or two that did not accurately communicate what it was I was trying to say. Pruff reading has never been my specialty. However, for my money, I send a text every time I can.

You can send text messages from the golf course or from your fishing boat on the lake. I have seen choir members texting during a church service, right out there in front of God and everybody. One youth minister sent out all of her correspondence to her youth through text messages. I have even sent a text message to my wife who was sitting across the table from me at a potluck supper: "Don't eat the potato salad. I found a hair in mine!"

Now they have taken texting a step beyond with something called Twitter. I do not twit. I don't know how to twit. What can a twit do that a text can't? Why is it every time I finally latch on to a craze and become cool with it, someone comes out with something new? Perhaps it is a vast right-wing conspiracy to disrupt the communications in our country.

I read recently where a college football quarterback tweeted that the opposing team's defense was not really that good. He took a beating, and his team lost big the next week. According to the reports, after getting pummeled by a 276-pound defensive tackle, the tackler told him to stop tweeting!

That's reason enough for me to stick to texting.

I foresee the day when everyone in the congregation will have a smartphone in their hand. The minister will text his message a paragraph at a time to his flock each Sunday, while probably sitting on the deck of a lake house somewhere sipping on a glass of sweet Southern ice tea and watching *Sportscenter* on his television.

In this case, give me that new-time religion.

Chapter 36
My Friend, the Pastor

In many ways, the parish ministry is one of the loneliest professions. I was taught in seminary and had reinforced in me by my superiors over the years that there must be a buffer zone between the minister and his flock. If you get too close to your people, it was argued, how can you be in effective ministry with them in times of crisis? You are to love your sheep, but from a distance.

I have concluded that the reason for this practice in the past was to hide the human imperfections of the pastor from her flock. We are supposed to be above reproach both personally and professionally. If your life's twists and turns bring out imperfections, you must somehow cover them up. You set the example, not Christ.

I have known a few ministers who set themselves up on such a pedestal, and their fall from such a self-appointed perch was a long and painful one. Americans love to place people on a pedestal and are most critical if they find their trust was misplaced.

It isn't that the ministers are full of moral turpitude. It simply means they are human beings who endured struggles, pain, and failures just like everyone else.

An older minister told me when I was just out of seminary that if I wanted to last in the ministry, I needed to make friends outside of the ministry. That is hard to do as a pastor. Ministers hang out with strange people. When your closest friends are other ministers and morticians, your social circle could stand to be widened a bit. I once asked a mortician friend of mine what the hardest part of his job was. He said trying to keep a smile off your face during a $15,000 funeral!

In the past, the district superintendent was the local minister's pastor and friend. When you needed to get away and unload, you could always go to them for a shoulder to cry on. Now you can't do that anymore. Any information you give them can and will be used against you in a church trial or during the appointment process. The age of confidentiality is over for the local pastor.

Many of the friends I have made in my adult life have been either the parents of my children's friends, through my wife's employment, or through social organizations I joined with fear and trepidation. Everywhere a minister goes, in all social circumstances, someone always wants to share a preacher's joke or a story about church they find amusing. The hardest part of a minister's job is to belly laugh over the same joke you heard twenty years ago. What you do fully becomes who you are in their eyes.

We have found over the years that when your relationship with church people changes, true friendships often develop. The best position in the world may be "the former pastor." You are no longer up on the pedestal as their pastor. They have put some other poor soul on your old pedestal. I heard a minister who was leaving an appointment tell his congregation he was no longer their pastor, but now he was their friend. I thought that it was a shame he could not have been both at the same time.

It is so ironic that most pastors are people persons but have so few personal friends. It breeds loneliness and depression.

I believe this gulf between pastor and congregation is one of the chief reasons ministers become burned out and leave the ministry. It is painful to admit that one of the things retirement offers a minister is the chance to become normal again. There are fewer people to impress with your piety. You can let your hair down, your beard grow, and your words flow without impunity.

So here are a few ideas. Let your pastors be human. If their children are typical PKs (preacher's kids), rejoice with them. They are just like you. They worry over the bills each month, like to watch the same television shows and movies you do, yell their lungs out for their favorite teams, have a personal life with their spouses, and tap the communion wine every now and then.

They are not there to be worshipped but to extend a hand to those in trouble, using their life's experiences as a means of empathy for you when troubles come your way.

Extend to your pastor the same grace you want them to extend to you. Befriend them because of who they are, not the position they hold.

They will be better pastors, and you will make a friend for life.

Chapter 37
I Want to Rock and Roll All Night
(As Long as I Am in Bed by Ten)

I became a big fan of the docusoap Gene Simmons Family Jewels. The show was about the domestication of one of my generation's biggest rock idols. The bass player from KISS is seen each week as just another dad, just another husband, who is facing some of the same day-to-day problems we do. He and his wife have raised two children, operated a business, and had plastic surgery together on the same show.

One thing I am coming to grips with is that my rock, pop, and country idols are getting old, which in turn has speeded up my own aging process.

The following singers and musicians are all now eligible for Social Security in our country:

Willie Nelson is ninety

Johnny Mathis is eighty-eight

Kris Kristofferson is eighty-seven

Smokey Robinson is eighty-four

Paul McCartney is eighty-one

Mick Jagger is eighty

Keith Richards is eighty

Doug Gray is seventy-five

Bruce Springsteen is seventy-four

I googled all of these folks to check that their ages were accurate. I noticed that beneath their names in the Google search, most had an entry with their name and the words plastic surgery behind it. Most are still performing somewhere across this land every weekend, but their concerts are sponsored by AARP and those walk-in bathtub people. Some are content to sit at home and draw their royalty checks along with their Social Security check each month.

I recently noticed I have developed a special kind of memory over the years. When I moved to a new place, whatever age a person was in that church when I got there, they are still that age in my mind today. It's hard to accept that children I baptized years ago now have teenagers of their own. I have discovered Facebook can sometimes bring this reality home to me in an abrupt way.

In my mind, David Cassidy will always be the teenager with the good-looking sister on television. Roy Clark will always be picking and grinning with his partner, Buck Owens. Doug Gray will always be one of those young boys from Spartanburg who helped introduce the world to Southern rock.

There are two exceptions in my mind on this list: Keith Richards and Willie Nelson. Keith is a walking, talking contradiction to everything my health teacher taught me in junior high. He looked sixty-five when he was thirty-five. Willie's appearance has not changed much in the last thirty years. I saw him in concert five years ago, and he played for two hours. Two hours was also the length of time his "goodbye fat" under his arm jiggled when he waved goodbye to all of us that night. They are both examples of better living through agriculture.

I find it hard to believe today's generation of entertainers will be held in as high esteem as these guys have been when they get to sixty-two and over. It's going to be hard to use your walker with your pants on the ground, for one thing. Hopefully rap music will have been replaced by something less offensive to sensitive ears. *American Idol* will be on season fifty by that time, and Ryan Seacrest will be in his eighties.

I won't be here to see it. I hope to join my own idols in the Heavenly Band by that time.

As the late Lawrence Welk said, a-wonderful, a-wonderful.

Chapter 38
I've Reached the Speed Limit

There are many memorable birthdays in a person's life. You turn six, and you're able to start the first grade. You turn thirteen and become an adolescent who knows more than their parents yet are so unsure of themselves. You turn eighteen and you can vote, and your parents can officially and legally kick you out of their house.

When you turn twenty-one, you finally can walk into a bar and restaurant and not worry about having to present a fake ID to purchase one of Milwaukee's finest. You are now seen by most people as an adult. You are responsible for your own decisions now.

Twenty-five is an important birthday for young men across our country. That is the day your car insurance, if you still have it, goes down dramatically. By twenty-five you are expected to have learned that just because your car will go eighty in a fifty doesn't mean it has to do so.

Five years later, you begin the decade birthdays. When you turn thirty, you tell everyone that it is just a number. You still feel like you did in college. Many of your friends are still the same. You are probably married, perhaps a parent, beginning to make progress in your career and feel like you have the world by the tail.

Ten years later, you turn forty. You still tell everyone it is just a number, but your back and knees are calling you a liar. Your children have just become teenagers, and you are being repaid for what you did to your own parents twenty-five years before. The career that was booming at thirty has slowed to a crawl because your job was outsourced to a guy in Pakistan. Some days it feels like the world has you by the tail.

Ten years later, you turn fifty. Your children are now in their sixth year of college, and they are still sophomores. Your hair has either turned gray or turned loose. You have endured orthopedic surgery, and there is a scar where your gall bladder used to be. A night out in the town is a quick trip to the frozen yogurt place where you eat fat-free, sugar-free yogurt and forego the nuts and toppings. Your second career has plateaued, and you realize the beach house on Malibu ain't happening.

Then a marvelous thing happens when you turn sixty-five. The merchandising world has determined that you are now eligible for senior discounts! I can order cheap coffee now in almost every restaurant. On my fifty-fifth birthday I asked for and received my ten percent senior discount at my favorite seafood place. I can now hit from the senior tees at the golf course without having to argue about my age. I can just whip out my AARP card and show my fellow golfers I have arrived at the magic age.

By sixty-five, your children have blessed you with grandchildren. You can sit back and smile as your grandchildren act out on their parents just like they did years ago on you. You can play with your grandkids and get them all wired up on sugary drinks and candy and take them back home to your children. While they bounce off the walls, you can go back to your home, turn on the television, lay back on the couch, and watch the commercials about burial insurance.

At sixty-five, you know you can't do what you used to, and for the most part you don't care. You get your exercise by continually walking through the house trying to remember what it was you got up to look for. Instead of bragging to your friends about your new car, you show off the fourteen-day pill dispenser you bought on sale at the drug store. Instead of counting the days till the weekend, you have started counting the days until retirement.

Finally, when you have arrived at sixty-five, you have come to the conclusion that there is no reason to bend over and pick up one item off the floor. You wait until there are several things down there you need, and you make the trip down there worthwhile.

They say that with age comes wisdom. With age also comes bad joints, new teeth, new attitudes, progressive lens glasses, cardigan sweaters, and argyle socks.

I guess that's enough on the subject. I must tug on my support hose and sandals and shuffle off to the pharmacy. It's time for my Metamucil and I ran out last night.

Chapter 39
PGA Champion

If there is one pastime that is almost synonymous with being a pastor, it has to be golf. I remember an older pastor telling me when I entered the ministry forty-five years ago that playing golf with the big wigs was a way to get "to the top." Like in business, the golf course was where friendships were forged and the real decisions were made.

It helped that I played golf already. My father would take me with him and his friends to play golf every Monday morning at the Peach Valley Golf Course near Spartanburg. I remember my parents buying my first set of golf clubs at J.C. Penney department store. The bag and clubs cost less than twenty-five dollars. I played with them until they started to rust.

When I was in seminary, four colleagues and I would always skip a day of Annual Conference to go play golf. That was an adventure we called "getting loose" and was always needed by the third day of Annual Conference. We would often see other ministers who decided a bad day at the golf course was better than a good day sitting in a meeting.

There was an organization called the Preachers Golf Association. We called it the PGA for short. Many members were pastors who always wanted to be a professional golfer but were never good enough. Being a preacher playing in their own PGA was as close as they would get.

Ministers of all denominations would play in those tournaments. You would often have a Lutheran minister drinking a cold beer riding in the same cart with a Church of God minister who was praying for his mortal soul. The surest way to ruin the Church of God minister's concentration was to throw a fake tantrum, shout a few choice words, and fuss and fume for a few minutes.

It worked every time I tried it. One Church of God minister wanted to take my hand and pray for me right there in the cart.

I beat him by eight strokes that day.

I played golf with my friend LaRue Cook almost every week for thirty years. He was a United Methodist minister who played more like a real PGA pro than I did. I beat him once in thirty years.

We played in Myrtle Beach one January when we had to wipe the sleet off our cart windshield. We played once in Anderson when the lake was frozen over near the eighteenth green.

Our time together was more like therapy than sport. We would discuss the joys and concerns going on in our life and talk about the other ministers who didn't play golf.

I have often used a round of golf as a fact-finding trip with church members. You can tell a lot about a person's personality on the golf course. I have found college-educated men who can't tell the difference between eight shots and six shots and whose math skills were atrocious. A few of my members have been color blind. They hit a white ball into the woods, but after claiming to find their ball, hit an orange one out. Some of the members would use this opportunity to tell me a joke I could use in church and more that I couldn't use in church.

A course pro once told me he hated to see me play with a particular foursome because it cost him plenty of bucks in lost beer sales. It seems my church members had a beer or six when they were not playing with the preacher.

If you know a minister who is a great golfer, he obviously isn't spending quality time in prayer, study, and fasting. If all his jokes start with "God, Jesus, and Moses were playing golf," he may be spending too much time on the driving range. If he divides all his study groups into groups of four, he may be spending too much time on the golf course. If he starts at the end of the line for covered dish dinners and asks if he can "play through," your minister may have a problem. If he describes his best friend and golf partner as a "hooker," he needs to stay in the study more.

Well, that's enough for now. I have a tee time in twenty minutes.

God bless.

Chapter 40
The Real Difference Between Men and Women

I remember watching a segment on television a few years ago where a college professor boldly proclaimed that men and women's brains work differently. He got a government grant to study this phenomenon for two years. He sat there with an idiotic smile on his face and said that yes, indeed, men and women think differently. He used a series of slides to show how one part of the female brain works more than the same part in the male. You would have thought he had discovered the cure for cancer.

Any person who has been married for more than two years could have told the professor that. Our tax dollars at work!

In my opinion, his discovery did put to rest that age-old dilemma between environment and heredity. We come into this world wired differently. Anyone who has ever raised a son and a daughter could tell you that.

My wife and I recently took our grandchildren clothes and shoe shopping. When we went into the shoe store, our grandsons both took off running for the fire engine ride at the back of the store. They started asking Papa for quarters and persisted in doing so until I got change for a ten.

My granddaughter, who is four, went immediately to the kids' shoe section. I fed quarters into the fire engine ride until both grandsons got motion sickness. My granddaughter, in the meantime, went from shoe to shoe. She had this strange glow in her eye. It was as if she was mesmerized by some higher power. I suggested a pair of nice-looking tennis shoes and she gave me that look, the same one her grandmother has given me over the past forty-five years, that says, "Are you kidding me?" After forty-five minutes we agreed on a pair of shoes that she said "made her look like a princess."

Our grandsons finally picked themselves up off the floor, spent two minutes picking out a pair of Nikes, and headed back to the fire engine.

Is there a shoe gene that is somehow repressed in a straight man's chromosomal make-up? I went home and counted my shoes. I had one pair of black dress shoes I call my funeral shoes. Every reverend has to have one of those. I had one pair of tennis shoes that cost me twenty-nine dollars. I have one pair of Harley-Davidson riding boots that are ten years old that I bought off eBay. I have two pairs of Crocs, one for the weekdays and one for Sunday. I have one pair of old brown shoes, which is my spare pair in case my black ones come apart. Six pairs of shoes total for the working man fulfills my wardrobe requirements.

I had to remodel our last parsonage so my wife would have a place to keep her shoes. I called it the Imelda Marcos Memorial Walk-In Closet. A hard hat was required by our insurance company for anyone who ventured into that room. I have to take part of the blame for all of this. I bought many of those shoes over the past thirty-five years. Like old age, the number of shoes just crept up on us I guess.

One thing I have never figured out is why a woman would suffer the pain she does to walk around in a pair of six-inch heeled shoes? The lady who doesn't wear them on a regular basis has the gait of a circus stilt walker, all the time trying to keep a look of grace and style on her face. The first thing she does when she gets in the car to go home is take them off. She walks in her stocking feet from the garage into the house complaining that her feet hurt. The shoes go back into the original box, which men never keep, until the next time she wears that same dress.

I look forward to the years ahead when my granddaughter will not be happy with discount shoe stores. With age has come the wisdom that you are better off tagging along, grunting accordingly but only when asked, and taking out the debit card at the appropriate time.

Her grandmother has taught me that, and I understand the premise.

Chapter 41
Hats, Mittens, and Bikinis

Author's note: An annual event shared by most United Methodist Youth Fellowships in South Carolina is a winter trip to the ski slopes of Western North Carolina and Tennessee. Southern kids, who love snow but hate cold weather, transport themselves in old church buses up Interstate 26 to the land of the sky. I wrote the following one February during the height of the snow ski season as my children prepared for their ski trip. It illustrates my total lack of timing and fashion sense.

Our youth are making their annual pilgrimage to the ski country of Tennessee this weekend. As many of you read this, young people will be sloshing down the slopes at breakneck speed. I can only hope our youth and their brave counselors all return home in one piece.

In preparation for this event, my children informed me they needed stocking hats and insulated gloves. Checkbook in hand, I left for the mall to try to find them.

What I found instead was heartache and insults. It was nine degrees the morning when I went shopping. I was wearing my overcoat and gloves to not freeze to death between the car and the mall's entrance.

When I entered the first store, all I could see in either direction was ladies swimsuits of all shapes and sizes. This was a bad omen.

The salesperson in sporting goods was very insulting to me. "Gloves and hats, this time of year? If you wanted gloves and hats you should have bought them in August or September."

In August and September, I was interested in buying shorts and swimsuits, not winter clothes and accessories. When I informed the salesperson of this, she replied that I should have planned ahead.

While I don't understand the timing of the fashion world, I do recognize good advice when I hear it. You do have to plan ahead in life because you never know what curves life is going to throw your way. Winter follows summer and fall every year. Troubles do come intermixed with the good times life has to offer us.

I have an uncle who reminds his family from time to time that we all need "to stay in a rigid state of flexibility." He is right. It wasn't raining when Noah started building the ark. You can't wait until the last minute to be prepared for the floods of life.

Here is God's plan of readiness for us.

Number one is prayer. Pray constantly. When the path of prayer becomes silent, troubles seem to appear larger than they are.

Second, have your house in order at all times. We don't know when the bridegroom is coming, but we know the wedding is planned.

Third, live expectantly. Be like the people who Christmas-shop in July. Prepare in advance for those events you know are coming up. People who live just for today are not usually prepared for what tomorrow will bring.

My mother ended up finding my sons their stocking hats and gloves. She said they were hiding behind the bikinis and sunscreen.

Chapter 42
Pardon Me While I Whip This Out

One of the duties of a pastor is to make almost daily visits to the hospital to care for his sick sheep. Some members think I get up every morning and head down to the hospital regardless of whether we have anybody from the church there or not. *Oh, contrare, mon ami.* There are sick people down there, in case you haven't noticed. Just the sight of doctors, nurses, and lab technicians makes my blood pressure rise.

I am a firm believer that if you stay in a hospital long enough, or visit there often enough, you will catch something. The fad lately has been the antibacterial dispensers they place in the lobby, by the elevators, in every patient's room, and in the bathrooms. If this is not confirmation enough that the hospital is Germ City, I don't know what is. It makes me want to wash my hands, face, neck, and other body parts every time I go and leave a hospital, just to make sure nothing unwanted rides back home with me.

Several years ago, I developed a MRSA staph infection from visiting the hospital. One mad dash for the lobby restroom left me with an orange-size infection that took a month and two surgical procedures to get rid of. Then my wife, the nurse, tells me it really isn't gone. It is hiding in my body waiting to make an untimely entrance sometime later in life.

When I was a younger minister, I was taught to always make physical contact with the patient. Hold their hand, pat their foot, sit at the foot of the bed, and reassure them that everything is going to be all right. I did so for years believing I had been taught well.

In the 1990s, the visitation experts changed their minds and theology. The patient's room was their domain, their home for a few days. Their privacy had already been invaded more than most could endure. (If you have never been in a hospital gown, your time is coming).

Now they tell you to keep your distance, always knock, and close the door securely when you leave. We are supposed to float in and float out, dripping words of assurance and kindness to all who inhabit that space.

This change of course came about at the same time as the rise in staph infections rose in virtually every hospital in the country. Because of this, I now treat every patient like they were in quarantine.

I have only been hospitalized once since I was a child. I had extensive shoulder surgery, which resulted in a change of my theology about pain killing medications. The nurse got my full and complete attention when she came in with this plastic container and told my wife if I couldn't "go" they were going to catheterize me. I learned if you can "go" under the influence of morphine lying flat on your back in a bed, you can do most anything in life. I went. The nurse left. All was good with my world until the next shot arrived four hours later.

A visit to the hospital for me is like playing the old game show *Let's Make A Deal*: you never know what might behind Door Number Three. It could be good news or somebody might have just been zonked. As a minister, you are supposed to be prepared for either contingency.

I always say a little prayer before entering a hospital. I ask God, "Help me say something that will cheer someone up or help someone today. And if possible, Lord, let me do it without catching what they have."

Then I wash my hands on the way in and out and hope he heard me.

Chapter 43
What Really Divides Us

My wife and I had the privilege of keeping our grandchildren one afternoon. At the time, they were six and four going on twenty-one. They came in, jumped on our couch, and said, "Papa we want to watch some cartoons."

That certainly seemed like a good idea to me. The large screen mounted on the fireplace could help entertain them, and I still enjoy a good cartoon every now and then.

I was shocked at what passes for cartoon entertainment back then, and I heard it is worse now. There were umpteen cartoon channels on the satellite to choose from. I admit most of the characters I had never heard of. The shows seem to be vehicles by which my grandchildren are encouraged to beg Papa for a trip to the toy store. My grandchildren received a creepy version of the old Easy-Bake Oven for Christmas. Instead of cooking cookies, they baked things shaped like brains and livers and such. I asked their father where they had seen such a thing, and he said, "Watching cartoons."

The Golf channel never had an advertisement for it I am pretty sure. If they did, I missed it.

I have concluded, after much thought, that the Baby Boomer generation, of which I am an AARP-card carrying member, is totally divided. It's not a red state-blue state thing. It goes back much farther than that. People my age were, and still are, divided over which cartoons they grew up watching. There were two categories of cartoons back in my day. You had those put out by Walt Disney such as Mickey Mouse, Donald Duck, Goofy, etc. Then you had those put out by Looney Tunes.

These, I pontificate, were the real cartoons of the day. You had Bugs Bunny, the Road Runner and Wiley Coyote, Yosemite Sam, Foghorn Leghorn,

Daffy Duck, and of course, Elmer Fudd.

In my entire life I have never found someone who liked both. I am a Looney Tunes guy, in more ways than one. I loved the Road Runner and the Coyote. I pulled for the coyote most of the time. I laugh out loud anytime I see a truck with the words ACME on the side of it. (If I have to explain this, you are obviously a Disney fan.) I grew up learning to imitate Foghorn Leghorn. "Well I say, well I say, there Boy!" and "I keep my feathers numbered for occasions like this" became part of my everyday speech.

For those of us who look for a deeper meaning in simple things, I could see a little of Groucho Marx in Bugs Bunny. However, it was still a cartoon meant for kids and for those of us who are still children at heart and intend to stay that way.

I have no desire to go to Disney World. I went to Epcot and wasted a bunch of money. Orlando has no appeal to me. It's hot, humid, and rains every afternoon from March until November at three o'clock. I'm not standing in line for two hours to ride anything short of a Lamborghini.

To me, Mickey Mouse is just a six-foot-tall rat. Goofy is just that, and Donald Duck has a speech impediment. Look at Walt Disney for a second. Supposedly he had his head frozen in a place out west somewhere in case they ever figure out how to attach it to another body and defrost him. I ask you, is that a role model for your children?

I say nay!

Let the talented voice of the late Mel Blanc make your children laugh like it did you. Find the Looney Tunes collections on DVD and entertain your children and rekindle your old memories.

For those of you who grew up Disney fans, I encourage you to repent and avoid central Florida. There's room in the Looney Tunes world I live in for all of you.

Chapter 44
The Golden Urn

My mother and father were married seventy-four years. They got married when they were seventeen, and they both lied about their ages so their parents wouldn't know about it. They went one town away and found an unsuspecting Methodist minister who married them. Afraid for their very lives, they traveled to Candler, North Carolina, where they honeymooned with my dad's grandparents until they got the word that my mother's mom was not going to kill them.

In 1990, the family gave them a very nice golden anniversary party at my Uncle Jim's house. Friends and family from all over came to take part in this special event. Food was prepared, cake was shared, and gifts were given.

It was almost a great time. My dad's sister, who was not my mother's favorite in-law, gave them the gift of a bronze funeral urn. My mom absolutely hated the idea of cremation. Being grilled with no frills was not how she wanted to go,

The urn went into a cabinet and never made an appearance. When she passed away and I started to clean up and sort through things, I found it. I don't share my mother's view of cremation. Being created is my only shot at having a flaming hot body. Besides, with the cost of a funeral today, I'd rather my family spend that money on themselves.

So, the urn now rests upon my high boy dresser. It's the last thing I see before I switch the television off at night and the first thing I see in the morning. It is a constant reminder that we all shall die when our time is up here on this rock. There is no escaping earthly death.

That urn is also a reminder to make every day count. Do something you like to do. Don't put off things until the time is right, for that day will never come. Take that trip. Eat that pork chop. Make amends with those you need to make amends with.

Most of all, get rid of the things that steal your joy. Stop caring what other people say and think about you. The only thing that matters is what God thinks about you, and he sent his son to be like us so that we can be like him.

That's how the God of all sees you. You are one of his.

We all need an urn in our life to make our priorities right.

Chapter 45
Playing Ball for Jesus

Author's note: I have several friends who are softball umpires, basketball referees, or football officials. I officiated basketball for more than sixteen years myself. It was much like preaching in that the people in the stands, or the pews, often felt like they could do a better job than I was doing. There is one thing all these people will tell you: Never umpire church softball games. People have been shot and killed over church softball games. The following is my experience at one of my appointments. It was a learning experience for which I received no college credits.

One of the outreach ministries my churches have offered over the years was church athletics. As a child, I remember the men of the church going out back after a covered-dish lunch and having a friendly game of softball on a hot summer afternoon. The women would sit in those steel Samsonite chairs, drinking Southern sweet tea or tart lemonade while their menfolk entertained themselves and the onlookers with a friendly game.

Those days are gone. I am not sure when it happened. It may have been during the Reagan years when church softball became a serious sport. While Ronnie was telling the Ruskies to tear down that wall in Berlin, the walls of sportsmanship and Christian fellowship were being eroded more and more with each softball season.

I was appointed to a small, two-point charge in the country during those years. One church had a softball team, and I looked forward to joining them for an evening of fun at the old ballpark once or twice a week. I soon found out this church of seventy or so people had tryouts for their church softball team. Tryouts! They recruited young men from all over the county to come play for the church team. I am sure there were guys on the team who had no idea where the church was, much less ever attended a service there.

They had three sets of uniforms. One set was for when they were the home team, one for when they were visiting, and one for the tournaments they played in. The coach very energetically told me he had convinced the boys to not drink during the games while they were playing in town. I assured him I and the bishop would appreciate that.

The next year one of the players, after much pleading from the minister, decided that he could not support the way the church softball team was conducted. He decided to have his own team and play in the open league. He invited his pastor to come and play with him and nine of his friends. I eagerly agreed. I thought this would make a statement to the church about the direction the church's team had been heading in and maybe would make them reconsider what type of team they would have in the future.

Those well-thought-out plans were demolished when I found out the sponsor for my new team was Verd's Ole Pub and Grill. I became their pitcher. Twice a week I put on my jersey, advertised their establishment, and played with the sinners.

This team behaved better than the church team. There were fewer temper tantrums, less cursing, and little drinking. It was almost like the games of old. The ladies would come out to cheer their men on, sipping on Southern sweet tea or hard lemonade, on a breezy summer night.

I knew I had become one of the guys when I threw a pitch that fell about five feet short of the plate. One slightly inebriated voice from our side said, "Say one more Hail Mary, Padre, and pitch it in there again."

My attempt at shaming the church into a more Christlike softball team failed. While I did get the folks to stop smoking in the church (this was in Marlboro County), they would not get out of the world of professional softball.

When I left this church, I stopped at the county line and did something very biblical. I shook the dirt out of my softball spikes and thanked God I was delivered from this place.

We aimed our U-Haul westward and left, knowing that there would be other softball teams in other places, but none like this one.

Chapter 46
Reading the Obits

I have developed an odd habit each morning. At least, it feels odd to me. I pick up my iPad and start browsing through the obituaries of at least five local newspapers from around the state. As a member of that organization of traveling vagabonds known as the Methodist clergy, I have personally said words over and buried hundreds of people all over the state. Some folks say I've buried more people than Forest Lawn. I'm close, sure enough.

Therefore, I have an unusual obsession with the dead. I read the obits to see if someone has died whom I might have ministered to over the years. I also read the obits from my hometown newspaper to see if any of the people I went to school with or grew up with have died.

Unfortunately, a good number of my classmates have passed on. I always read the entire obituary because it concerns me that people my age are in the obituary column. I am always hoping their obit will end by asking people to contribute to the American Cancer Society, Alcoholics Anonymous, or Al-Anon. I hold to the thought that if someone my age bought the farm, it was because they indulged in some bad habit that I don't, and it caused their much-too-early demise.

If I don't see that, I am hoping they were killed by a freak chemical accident, in a plane crash, a bolt of lightning, or some act of nature. If none of these are the culprit, I pray they died of lead poisoning administered by a jealous husband, wife, or girlfriend.

Anything but old age or natural causes.

As I have read thousands of obits over the years, I have found a trend unique to our Southern culture: Nicknames in the obits. I recently saw the obit of a man who died whose name was listed and then in parentheses it said, "Jim Dandy." Neither his first nor middle name was Jim, and after reading his obit, I seriously doubt he was a dandy.

Big Daddy, Junior, Butch, Buster, and Toots are nicknames that show up on a regular basis. I saw a man whose given names were Robert and James but whose nickname was "Eunice." There is a story there that needed to be expounded on. Interestingly, his wife's name was not Eunice.

There are always plenty of Roberts called Bob, Elizabeths called Lib, Bettys called Bette, and Harolds called Harrys. Those are commonplace. The one that was set apart from the rest was a guy nicknamed "Lover Boy." He had seven sons and four daughters. Every son had a different last name. He had dozens of grandchildren and great-grandchildren. The last line of his obit said, "He loved everybody." Apparently, as often as he could!

So I read on each morning trying to make sense of this thing called life. No matter how long you live or what you accomplished, everyone's life can be summed up in three column inches or less.

So here is my obit. I wrote it myself. It pretty much sums it all up.

Kim (Big Mac) Strong died last week of natural causes (heart attack in a fast-food line). He is survived by one long-suffering wife, two children, five grandchildren, and a host of astonished and bewildered relatives. He was born in Spartanburg because he wanted to be near his mother. He served, and was served by, numerous churches in South Carolina, some of which are still in business today.

He served in the military and helped defend Myrtle Beach against the Arabs during the first great Arabian war. He was a man of many passions, most revolving around barbecued food and things that go fast and make a lot of noise.

His services will be Saturday from one until five p.m. Five different Baptist preachers have been asked to participate because he wanted to make sure someone would be sorry he died.

His ashes will be carried to the Carolina-Clemson football game each fall with the hopes of a Gamecock victory and a Tiger defeat.

Instead of flowers, you are asked to contribute to The Ronald McDonald House, as it was one too many hamburgers that killed him.

That pretty much sums it up. Preachers like having the last word each Sunday morning, and I'm not going to let a little thing like death change that.

See you later, or see you in the obits.

Chapter 47
The Dentist from Hell and Bad Karma

I grew up with a tremendous fear of the dentist. The only dentist I had for the first eighteen years of my life caused me more sleepless nights as a teenager than the homecoming queen ever did. He was a churchgoing, God-fearing man. He was well known in the community and well-liked by everyone who did not have him as a dentist.

He was not a believer in painless dentistry. If you came in with a cavity, he made the experience as horrible as he could, while telling you if you brushed your teeth and quit drinking soft drinks, you would not have a problem with your teeth.

He is the reason dentists started wearing masks. It was not to avoid germs. It was to avoid being picked out of a lineup down at the station house should he ever kill or seriously maim his patient.

The only dentist worse than him was his intern. I had an emergency trip to the dentist when I was in college. I was never told that wheat, barley, and fried foods was a deadly combination for your teeth. I had a tooth that needed a filling, and the intern was the only guy there.

He was better with the needle than his teacher. Things were going well until he said you need a root canal. I wasn't sure what that was, but I found out. It went fairly well considering I had a gallon of Novocain in my jaw.

I had to return to see him two more times. I dutifully returned to the office, walked to the chair with confidence and sat down. The technician wrapped that blue bib around my neck, uncovered the tray of torture tools and left me alone to ponder my fate.

The dentist came in, sans mask, tilted me back, took his Black and Decker power drill and started drilling my tooth out. I gently tapped him on his arm, and he stopped long enough for me to ask him this question: Are you not going to give me a shot? His answer set back dentistry a hundred years. He said "No, the only way I know I got all the nerves is when it stops hurting."

He proceeded to use his instruments to jerk out live nerves from my jaw. They landed on my cheeks with regularity. My wife, who was my fiancé then, heard me yelling in the lobby. She was amazed that a pre-ministry student knew words like that.

I had to return a third time. I sat in the parking lot, took one of my mother's "nerve" pills with a shot of Jack Daniels whiskey, and went in to finish this root canal from hell.

I did not return to see any dentist for over five years. The girl who cleaned my teeth kept giving me dirty looks as she used a hammer and chisel to clean away five years' worth of wear.

I found to my delight that not all dentists were like those two. I have the best dentist in the world now. He is the son of two of our friends, and he has been virtually painless to go see. The first time he brought the shot and drill out, I told him I would hold him by his crotch, and if he didn't hurt me, I wouldn't hurt him. He laughed and said he didn't think that would be necessary, and he was right. I never felt a thing. I actually look forward to seeing him now.

But I have never forgotten the Minglea brothers who used to treat me. One night around eleven, my youngest son called us to tell us he had been in an accident. He was fine, but the car he was driving went into a ditch. He said not to worry, that it wasn't my car, it was his friend's car. He said he was driving his friend's father's Lexus. I started to admonish my son until he called the car owner's name.

It seems he was a dentist. He was the same dentist who performed that painful root canal.

My son had a hard time figuring out why I was laughing hysterically in the middle of the night at his news. Instead of a lecture I told him not to worry about it and to get in his car and drive safely home.

Maybe there is something to that karma thing. If not, God surely has a wicked sense of humor. Either way, I liked it.

Chapter 48
The Ugly Old Red Couch

Author's note: My beloved United Methodist Church stands today on the brink of splitting into at least two denominations. There is bitterness among God's children over whether to accept some of his children into the ministry. The division is devasting to some and liberating to others. It is not the first great division I have dealt with in the church, however. Here is another division I dealt with years ago that was just as bitter and just as divisive.

There have been many great divisions in the church over the past two thousand years. Orthodoxy versus neo-orthodoxy, Catholicism versus the Protestant Reformation, immersion versus sprinkling, and church barbecues versus the dreaded spaghetti dinner. Four years of college and three years of seminary did not adequately prepare me to address some of the aforementioned issues.

Nothing prepared me, however, for the greatest division in the church I ever faced. I called it "The Schism of the Ugly Old Red Couch." It happened far away from the lights of the big city where most new ministers ply their trade.

I had two United Methodist churches in rural Marlboro County. On a clear day you could see between the two churches. These two churches shared a pastor and a parsonage but little else. One was a small church dominated by a large family membership. The other was a smaller church dominated by a smaller family membership.

Both churches struggled to meet their local bills and to pay their conference apportionments. Their parsonage was rustic. Two kerosene heaters and a fireplace provided warmth for the four of us for two long winters. Each fall and winter afternoon, I would chop wood and store it under a cover so we could have a fire each morning to warm by. We twice found rattlesnakes in our washroom and carport.

This appointment was described to me as a "great opportunity."

The great event called Moving Day, arrived and that evening a couple from the smaller church came to the parsonage. We thought they were there to welcome us to the community. Wrong! They came to show us which pieces of fine furniture came from their church, and which came from the "other" church.

They pointed to one ugly red couch some people would call an antique in the living room. Great Uncle Dead and Buried But Not Forgotten had donated that to the parsonage years before his untimely departure for the Promised Land.

They let me know in no uncertain terms that when this charge separated and they got their own pastor, they wanted this couch back. They pointed out several other pieces of furniture, but this couch was the center of their existence as a church, and it had to be returned upon the death of this unnatural ecclesiastical marriage between the two churches.

I was brokenhearted. In just ten short hours I had become obsessed with this couch. We had a twenty-two-month-old son and another on the way and had just moved two hundred miles into a house that was falling in. We were living off $14,000 a year. Yet the most important thing for me to remember was the ownership of the red couch.

Several months later, I asked the unofficial chairman of the board of the smaller church why these two churches had not merged into a bigger church. He got indignant and said because a member of the other church had punched him in the nose. I asked him when this had occurred, and he said it was in the third grade. He was now seventy-six years old.

I'm glad he wasn't bitter.

I served a two-year sentence until I was paroled from this appointment and sent to a three-church charge. These churches are still in existence but no longer connected. I'm very sure that couch had something to do with it.

I am very sure that in the future, the new theologians will consider our divisiveness over our current issues to have been as stupid as this church's desire to retain this couch.

Chapter 49
The Problem with America, as I See It

Political ads have started to slowly infiltrate my television set. I have avoided both CNN and Fox News, which isn't fair and balanced by the way, to simplify my life and reduce my stress level. I read eleven newspapers a day online. I'd much rather read the news and study people's rhetoric than actually have to hear it. Hearing it riles me up. It makes me send money and support issues that I discover later might not have been worthy of my time or money.

I grew up in the South, the son of textile workers. As a de facto lint head, many of my political beliefs came from hearing my parents, primarily my father, rant about politics. My dad would often watch the early cable shows and yell back retorts to the commentators as they spewed their venom toward each other.

My dad had cancer surgery in 1991, and it was not until a couple of years later that he started yelling at the television again. That's when we discovered he had been in a depression since his surgery. We thank Pat Buchanan for snapping my dad out of his doldrums.

My parents started talking about the dangers of textile imports in the mid-1970s. My dad said one day the mills would all close down because of those overseas imports.

My dad was not only an amateur television commentator, but he was also a prophet. The mill he and my mother worked in is now closed and dismantled. The life they, and thousands of other people, knew suddenly was gone.

I blame half of this problem on Walmart. I remember when Walmart came to town. They proudly displayed a banner when you came through the door that said, "Made in America." My how things have changed. The sign today would have been, "Made in China." I remember when Ross Perot was running for president, he talked about that "giant sucking sound coming from the south." He was trying to warn us our jobs would go to Mexico.

Ross was right, but his direction was wrong. If there was a sucking sound coming from Mexico, there is now a black hole blasting away from China. The strange thing is if the computer I am typing this on, which was made in China, develops a problem, I must talk to a person named Buffy in Pakistan to get help.

While this is going on, Americans are standing in unemployment lines and living on food stamps because the jobs they used to have took a permanent trip abroad. We have made the poor in other countries richer by making our own people poorer, all in pursuit of higher corporate profits.

You might wonder why I have taken off on this tangent. We had a patriotic program at church recently. Lee Greenwood's song "God Bless The USA" was played, and we all were given little American flags to wave while we sang along. When I looked down at the flag in my hand, I noticed these words imprinted on the flagstick: "Made in China."

That ain't right.

I don't care who you are, that ain't right.

Here's how we fix this problem. Buy American. You will have to look a little harder to find these items, but there are still people making things in our country. Support politicians who not only want to level the playing field on trade issues, but who want to tilt the field toward the home team.

Charity begins at home, and it's time we take care of our own people and put our folks here back to work.

Let's make "Made in China" obsolete. Let's make it chic to buy items made in Montgomery, Alabama, and Charleston, South Carolina, and Rapid City, South Dakota, and Enfield, Connecticut.

In the seventies at the height of the gas problem, folks were saying, "Let the Arabs eat their oil."

This may not be politically correct, but it's time to fix the problem, not worry about the wording.

Chapter 50
Hand-Me-Down Grace

I grew up in a large family. I know that may sound puzzling to those who know I was the only child my parents conceived. My parents raised my mom's three youngest sisters, and I came along a little late in life for them.

Fortunately, I had a big bunch of first cousins. I had a few older male cousins and a few younger male cousins. My mother and my aunts devised a system of hand-me-downs that kept us clothed for the first ten or so years of my life. My older cousins usually wore a size or two larger than I did. I was usually a size or two larger than my younger male cousins. We had a clothing chain long before Walmart came along.

What came down to me were usually blue jeans and long pants. I wore them until the knees developed serious grass stains or became holey jeans. My mother, who was a seamstress, would cut them off and make short pants out of the worst ones.

When they became too snug, they went down to my youngest cousins, who wore them until they became boxers or briefs for my cousin at the end of the chain. Obviously, he didn't get to go out much.

This was fine when I was younger, but it became an embarrassing fact that I was wearing somebody else's clothes. It made me feel poorer than we were. However, denim was denim, and we wore those Billy the Kid jeans until the label just said "Bill."

I grew up swearing I would never wear hand-me-down clothes again. I lived that way until I retired and discovered the joy of eBay. I had always admired people who wore Tommy Bahama and Ralph Lauren shirts. I bought my shirts on sale at Belk's at the end of the season and put them in the back of the closet until spring or fall arrived.

In the last year I bought nearly twenty Tommy Bahama and Ralph Lauren shirts from eBay. The twenty shirts cost me about $200 instead of one new Tommy Bahama shirt that sells for $125 to $150. Every other week, two more shirts came in, and I didn't care that somebody else had worn them and then put them up for sale. Another hand-me-down, but this time I did the choosing and buying.

Then my attitude changed again. I bought a nice shirt from eBay that had another guy's name sewn into the shirttail. My imagination began to run wild. Maybe he had his name on his shirts because he used a laundry and didn't want one of his prize shirts lost. That would be a responsible thing to do.

Then I remembered when my dad was in the nursing home. They would sew his name on his clothes so they could keep up with his clothes at the laundry. I gave his clothes to Goodwill after he passed except for one pair of socks with his name on them. When I am having a low day, I take them out of my sacred sock drawer, put them on, and somehow feel closer to him. Only I know, and that comforts me.

The man who owned this shirt paid the expensive price for a new shirt, and somehow it ended up in my hands for nearly nothing.

That is how grace is offered to us. Jesus paid the expensive price for it with his life on a cross. When he was raised from the dead, your name and everyone's name who has ever lived or will ever live had their names sewn onto his graveclothes. His grace has been handed down to us and is available not to the highest bidder, but totally free.

I don't know the man whose shirt I bought, but I will think about him every time I put it on. It will be a reminder to me that my name is on something much more special than a shirt.

Holiday Reflections

Chapter 51
Happy New Year and Pass the Greens

New Year's Day is always an interesting day in the life of a church. It's the start of a new business year for most churches, and folks get a new box of offering envelopes to start paying on those new pledges. Some churches have Watch Night services on New Year's Eve. I had a few of those years back but stopped when I learned of a church member who was hit and killed by someone who had been drinking a little more of the communion wine than we had.

New Year's Eve at our house usually involved waking my wife up at midnight to get a sleepy kiss as I brought in the New Year with Dick Clark from Times Square. Spending New Year's Eve there was on my original bucket list until I saw an interview with a NYC policeman who said you had to be there by nine and stand three hours in the cold and/or rain and/or sleet until midnight without the aid of restrooms. A man my age prefers the couch, the fridge, and his own bathroom.

I read that in Japan on the stroke of midnight on New Year's Eve, most people swallow seven grapes for good luck. If you did not choke to death, it was a sign that you could expect a prosperous new year.

New Year's Day brings out a lot of superstitions in Southern folks. We always have black-eyed peas and collard greens, with some type of pork thrown in. The black-eyed peas are supposed to represent coins and the collards dollar bills. Pork represents the clogged arteries we intend to die with. Since I don't eat greens, all I have ever received was pocket change.

In our house, the new diet starts after the peas and greens are devoured. Each year we start with the best of intentions. Whether it is the Atkins Diet,

The South Beach Diet, or Weight Watchers, we eagerly begin our new program determined to lose the fifteen pounds we have added since Thanksgiving. My diet made it to Labor Day last year, which was a personal best for me. Usually, Valentine's Day is a noble goal.

New Year's Day in our house means that is the day the Christmas tree comes down. First the hanging decorations, then the lights, then the tree limb by limb. My wife collects Santas of all shapes and forms, and they go back into their boxes for their eleven months of hibernation. The angels fly away to their corners of the basement to watch over us until Thanksgiving comes again.

I always like to watch the network news on New Year's Eve. They show pictures of folks who have passed away in the last year. Lately more and more people who were part of my generation have been added to the list. Rock and roll is here to stay, but the old rockers have joined that eternal band in the heavens. A schoolmate or two of mine has also joined the heavenly choir in the past year.

If I am still alive to watch the video obits each New Year's, that is a sign that God has left me here because he has more for me to do. More sermons to preach, more visits to make, more songs to be played and sung, and more committee meetings to hold. It means he is giving me another year to love my wife, children, grandchildren, church members, and friends. It means I have another opportunity to do those things I have always wanted to do and to finally do the things I have put off for another day.

So happy New Year. Toast the New Year with a Diet Coke, or beverage of your choice, and thank God for letting you see another year. Who knows what great things this year can bring?

Chapter 52
Easter Sunrise, or Jesus Was Still Alive at 11 a.m.

One of the first questions I was asked when I arrived at a new church wasn't a question but a statement: We have an Easter Sunrise Service here! You are going to have Easter sunrise services, aren't you? My reply was "Yes! I look forward to that."

I lied. I don't know of any minister who can truthfully say they look forward to a sunrise service. We are late risers, most of us. We have seen many more sunsets than we have sunrises. One of my goals for my remaining years is to keep that fact an important part of my everyday life.

I have set 7 a.m. as the official Easter sunrise time in my churches for the last twenty years. I don't care what time the Weather Channel says it occurs— the sun doesn't rise at my church until 7 a.m. I have often pontificated on the fact that Jesus was just as risen at 11 a.m. as he was at 7 a.m. Even his own followers had a hard time recognizing him that early in the morning. I bet by 11 everyone would have been wide awake and nobody would have thought he was the gardener.

I have "enjoyed" some unusual experience at sunrise services. Many years ago I served a church situated on the main highway coming out of Myrtle Beach, South Carolina. At 7, my faithful were standing up in the parking lot next to the highway getting ready to sing when a South Carolina Highway Patrolman pulled over a family of five and two dogs trying to find their way back to Ohio. It seems they were in a special hurry to get there and were breaking the speed limit. With his blue lights flashing and siren blowing, he pulled them over forty feet from where we all were standing. He wrote them a ticket for the last hundred dollars they had left after a week of miniature golf and seafood buffets and sent them on their way to Cleveland.

You never know what kind of weather you are going to get on Easter Sunday. I always felt sorry for the ladies who spent good money to buy sleeveless, colorful summer dresses for Easter Sunday and woke up to find it was thirty-eight degrees with a twenty mile per hour wind. Many sunrise services were punctuated by Southern belles shivering their way through four verses of "Up From The Grave He Arose."

I remember one year when a typo in the newsletter caused much undue excitement on Easter Sunday morning. The newsletter was supposed to say "We will have a churchwide breakfast following the Easter sunrise service at 7:30." What it said instead was a churchwide breakfast would follow the Easter Sunrise service, and the cost will be $7.30." We almost had to cancel Easter that year because of the civil uprising following this within the ladies circles.

All of this could have been avoided by cancelling the Easter sunrise service and having a church brunch following the 11 a.m. service.

This year we are having a sunrise service at 7 followed by free doughnuts at 7:30 and a joint service at 10:30. This will be followed by families going home and serving a spiral spliced ham in honor of the King of the Jews and Lord of our Church.

Follow this up with a short egg hunt and a long nap.

Happy Easter, everyone!

Chapter 53
Tricks or Treats

It's Halloween time again. All of us over fifty will make a run to the store to buy a big bag of candy for the kids who don't come around anymore. Somehow in the last thirty years, Halloween has become an adult holiday. Adults go out and rent or buy incredibly expensive, and sometimes risqué, costumes to wear to their favorite watering hole for a night of alcohol and indigestion-causing foods. Next to Christmas, we spend more money on Halloween in the ole USA than any other holiday.

It wasn't always this way. I remember the great anticipation I had as a child as the thirty-first of October drew near each year. I had a great Casper the friendly ghost costume one year. I dressed up as my favorite spook, and my mother would walk me completely around the neighborhood as I made my hollow threat of extortion to our neighbors. My reward was enough candy to cause multiple cavities and the onslaught of Type 2 diabetes. I would go home and spread my "catch" out on the table and slowly start devouring it all one piece at a time.

As I grew older, I outgrew the costume and went out with only a mask to hide my true identity. I knew in my hometown there was an ordinance that prohibited kids over the age of twelve from wearing a mask. It seems some older folks decided a Halloween mask was a good cover for someone robbing a gas station.

This was about the same time some idiot in our community put a razor blade in an apple. The rumor was that some child had split their face open on the razor blade and had been rushed to the hospital. Nobody knew who this kid was, but nobody wanted a smile like the Joker's. Not wanting to take any chances, the local hospital started offering their X-ray equipment to the public each Halloween as a means of checking for foreign objects in their kids' Halloween bags.

This was the time Halloween changed. Parents went from following their children in the car to becoming personal bodyguards for their little goblins. The result was that fewer and fewer children started coming and knocking on our door each October. The Halloween candy would still be there for the Easter Bunny to recycle.

Halloween carnivals became the in thing to do until the conservative churches and the ACLU began battling over the holiday and public funding. Some churches used this children's holiday as a chance to have haunted houses based on their concept of hell. Their purpose was to scare children out of hell into heaven. This usually worked about as long as the Halloween candy lasted.

The Halloween carnival became the fall festival. Kids quit trick or treating, and adults became much more interested in the holiday than the kids were. I could hear the death knell for the lonely trick or treater being sounded as half drunk, half clothed adults hurried by on their way to their parties.

Each Halloween, however, my wife and I still go and buy a huge bag of candy in hopes that someone will still ring our doorbell. This year I suggested to my wife that we buy candy that we don't like. Neither one of us needs to add four pounds of sugar to our waist this year, and with Thanksgiving coming up we must start pacing ourselves.

I still remember one Halloween when I was in the fourth grade. I got sick the day before Halloween, and my mother took me to see the doctor. I got a shot, of course, and cried all the way home. It wasn't the shot that caused the tears. He told my mother to not let me go out on Halloween.

I begged and pleaded with my mother who finally relented. She went with me to six doors on our street. I got a little candy and some great medicine because she did not do what the doctor said, which was a first. There have been nearly sixty Halloweens since then, but that is the one that still means the most.

So turn your porch lights on, put a bowl of candy next to the door, and see who comes to your door this year. It will probably be a small child, holding onto the hand of a grandparent, who is getting more out of the night than their grandchild is.

Chapter 54
Would You Water My Aluminum Tree Please?

The day after Thanksgiving is a special day for my family. That is the day we always either go up into the attic or down into the basement to retrieve the Strong Family Christmas Tree.

After lugging the tree into the living room we try to read the instruction sheet, which was written in a size two font, and put the tree together. It is always a hassle. Bending and shaping a tree's limbs is something that is better left to the good Lord to do. We meticulously start with the bottom limbs, bending and fluffing each limb so it looks as natural as a plastic tree can look. By the time we get to the upper limbs, they are getting a quick shake and are shoved into place.

It used to not be this way. From the time I was just a wee lad—well, a younger lad—we always had a live tree. I remember my mom and I getting the tree on the first Friday in December, and we would put it up on Friday night. We used light bulbs about the size of a Coke bottle and strung icicles all over it. When it looked just so, we would place the star up on the top and light her up.

Artificial trees back in those days were not green; they were silver. My grandmother had the greatest silver Christmas tree. She had the revolving light wheel that sat on the floor and shot red, green, and blue light up on the tree. People would drive for miles to see her tree in her front window.

Folks today would call that a redneck Christmas tree. Even so, I went on eBay just to see if I could find one. They were three hundred dollars with the wheel! They were called antiques, since only those of us who are antiquated can remember them. I wanted the tree, but with age comes wisdom, and I put my credit card back in its holster.

A church I served once had a big debate over whether we were going to put a real or artificial tree up in the sanctuary. It got ugly really quick. The conservationist in the church thought the idea of cutting down a perfectly good tree and killing it off in a month was a horrible idea. One person even asked the group, "What would Jesus do?" Since Jesus was Jewish, he would tell them to light a candle instead.

One lady pulled out an old brochure printed by the Methodist Episcopal Church South in 1935 that said nothing artificial could be used in the sanctuary. No silk flower or plastic tree would get by her discerning presence. A church member who only came to church on Christmas continued to donate a tree from his acreage. A city ordinance required us to have a fire extinguisher in the church with a person who knew how to operate it in case the real tree ignited. He sat on the front pew, armed and ready, but thankfully it was never used.

Our tree is not only artificial, but it even came with the lights on it. Of course, the second year we used it, of the lights were not working because our cat had chewed through the wires, evidently when the lights were off. The cat is still living, but the tree is on life support.

For twenty years, my dream has been to simply throw a sheet over the tree, unplug it from the wall, and carry it down to the basement. That could work this year since it is the first time in thirty years we have a basement. Instead of putting the tree back up, I am going to vacuum it off, hit it with some Armor All, and put it back in the living room next season.

That is my Christmas wish. What is yours?

Chapter 55
What I Really Want for Christmas

Every year on Thanksgiving after the food has been consumed and the Cowboys and Lions have lost their traditional Turkey Day games, my wife asks me a question. What do you want for Christmas?

I never have an immediate answer. It's not that there aren't material things I would want to have. There are. I just don't want to spend three years paying for them at this point in my life.

Besides, I have learned that things do not hold the answer to my real needs, my real desires, my real wants in life. It took me sixty years or so to have that moment of enlightenment.

What do I really want for Christmas this year? A few simple things would be nice.

First, sleep would be nice. More of it and better sleep is what many people will tell you they need most in life. I sleep with a CPAP machine, and it helps me sleep until somehow it gets turned sideways on my head and it sounds like a 1971 Chevelle rushing by your ear. Sleep is good.

Knowledge would be a wonderful gift. Not book knowledge—I've been to school long enough. Ask my wife. I want the knowledge that my children and grands are going to be all right and have a long and happy life if their overweight, stressed out, blood-pressure-pill-popping father buys the condo this year. I would also like to know if I'm going to be here to wake up next Christmas. If not, the gift giving might be cut back some this year.

More time is something a lot of folks say they wish they had more of. However, the last time I checked, we all have twenty-four hours in a day. I don't need more time. I just need to use it better. That time management course I took at Emory in 1981 is just a memory.

As you experience more time here, you also come to know who your real friends are in life. My wife and I have learned that lesson the hard way at several places during our lives together.

Mostly, I just want people to get along. We need to quit living on the fringes of life and learn to meet in the middle. We need to enjoy life and each other and move our church and country forward.

Finally, pass a law that all men's pants come with expand-a-belt features. I'm not talking spandex. Spandex isn't for everyone. You know, just in case too much of the Christmas gatherings hang around into the new year. Or next Christmas.

No, keep the socks, the ties, and the golf balls for another year. I don't need more of those things. I need things even Amazon can't bring. Gold, frankincense, and myrrh were nice gifts, but I bet Joseph and Mary would have traded them all for a good night's sleep and a little peace of mind.

Chapter 56
Please Daddy, Don't Get Drunk this Christmas and Other Songs of the Season

The Christmas season must be upon us, because it is seven weeks before Christmas and the radio stations have started playing Christmas music. I was in a local store the week after Labor Day when I heard their PA system playing "Sleigh Ride." It's hard to think about Christmas when it is ninety degrees outside, but advertisers continue to start the Christmas shopping season earlier each year.

The local stations here started playing the sounds of the season right after Halloween. They just play Christmas music on Friday nights and all day Saturday. I think they are in cahoots with the malls. As you are out shopping, they want to get you into the Christmas spending spirit.

You know what, it works! I went into the bowels of our basement in pursuit of our Christmas music box. I found it under the Santa collection and the Christmas village boxes we have not opened in ten years. I dragged it up the steps, cleaned off the dust and the moving tags, and opened my yuletide treasure. We have been buying and collecting Christmas music for the past forty-five years. Our very first Christmas music was a cassette tape of Mitch Miller and his orchestra. It has survived a dozen moves and forty-five Advent seasons.

Our taste in Christmas music grew as its platforms began to diversify. Our collection of tapes included a Kenny Rogers Christmas album. He made this tape before his plastic surgery made him look like the love child of The Joker and Charlie Chan. We bought another Rogers tape as he and Dolly Parton recorded together. We bought that tape while I was in seminary and we were trying to live in two places and pastor two churches on the side. We did not have much money that year, but we added it to our Christmas collection.

With the introduction of the compact disc came a myriad of possibilities. We bought a disk by Kokomo Jo. It was a recording of Caribbean Christmas music. Santa Claus was on a jet ski holding a margarita. That's my kind of Christmas celebration.

We have most of the Christmas classics now. Bing Crosby sings "White Christmas" at our house each year. Nat King Cole sings about chestnuts roasting on an open fire even though I would not know a chestnut if it fell off the tree and hit me in the head. Doc Severinson and the old Tonight Show Band recorded the best version of "Sleigh Ride" I have ever heard. I remember them playing that on the *Tonight Show's* last live show before Christmas one year. That was back when the *Tonight Show* was funny.

About thirty years ago, novelty Christmas songs began to infiltrate the airways. "Grandma Got Run over by a Reindeer" became a Christmas staple in many houses. My personal favorite was Robert Earl Keene's "Christmas in the Family." I have lived out that song several Christmases in my own family.

John Denver's "Please Daddy Don't Get Drunk this Christmas" was a favorite at our house for years. It has been recorded at least a hundred times since the late Denver recorded his version. When I was a small child, I got a whiff of that special drink my dad and uncle had every year at Christmas. I did not know what it was, but that smell lingered in my memory as a part of Christmas.

I found out later that the smell was coming from a shot of Crown Royal. It even comes in a purple bag, signifying its part in Advent at my house. Its smell still brings back Christmas memories to me. Even in April.

We have bought at least one new Christmas recording each year we have been together. The box is getting heavier every Christmas season. This year I bought an R&B Christmas favorites CD. James Brown is singing his version of "Sleigh Ride." Nothing goes together better than James Brown and Christmas. His CD made me want to jump back and kiss myself.

I hope this Christmas season will be a blessing for you. Unfortunately, I have been bad this year and I have it on good authority that I'm getting nuttin' for Christmas.

Oh, well. Merry Christmas!

Chapter 57
Christmas on Layaway

I just finished my Christmas shopping for my wife. I found everything she asked for, and a few things she didn't, online. I picked out my items, browsed through the clearance sections for any good deals, imputed my credit card number, and hit submit. Everything will be shipped to my office so I can help Santa hide them until Christmas morning.

My, how things have changed. When I was a child we did not even have Walmarts to shop at during Christmas. In my community, the wealthier people shopped for their children's Christmas items at F. W. Woolworth and Sears and Roebuck downtown. Sears and Roebuck had a catalog that often ended up in an outhouse someplace. My folks never ordered from a catalog because they wanted to be able to see and touch what they were buying.

In my community, we had a lady named Doris Jones who operated a toy store in her renovated basement. It was full of toys from the floor to the ceiling. It was as if Santa had branched out from the North Pole itself and settled in South Carolina!

Because there were so many children and so few toys, my mom told me I could pick out only three toys every year at Christmas. I would wander from aisle to aisle with eyes glazed over with the joy of Christmas receiving. Every year I would end up picking out some type of toy gun. I usually picked out a gun that made a lot of noise. One year I got one that even had smoke coming out of the end.

One year, Mrs. Jones had the perfect gift. It was a shooting gallery. It was a smaller version of the ones I had seen at the county fair and in Myrtle Beach. It shot small metal balls at enclosed objects and played music and flashed light. What else could a ten-year-old boy want?

I counted the days until Christmas. The last few day crawled by. Finally, Christmas Eve arrived, and we packed up and went to my uncle's house for Christmas Eve dinner. After food and caroling and hours of laughter, we would return home and I would attempt to go to sleep.

I jumped out of bed the next morning and ran into the living room to enjoy my cherished treasure. What followed was a life-changing experience. The shooting gallery was there under the tree but it didn't work. It didn't work! Any ideas I had about there being a Santa went down the tubes that morning. Santa would not bring a broken toy to a good boy like me!

In an effort to calm my broken heart, my parents made me a promise they lived to regret. They told me that in the morning I could go back to Jones Toyland and pick out anything I wanted. What I wanted wouldn't work. How could anything replace that?

The day after Christmas, we were at her house at nine o'clock. After twenty minutes of aimless wandering, I found the worst gift she had that a parent could buy their kid: a set of drums! I picked out the drums and reminded my parents of their promise. They went home with us in the back of my dad's Buick.

I beat on those drums for months. Early in the morning and late at night I played. After school and on weekends, I worked on my drumming technique. I can only imagine now as an older adult how my parents must have regretted that decision: "You can have anything you want." Everything I got for Christmas after that I am sure was tested prior to Christmas morning.

I have shared this story with my sons so my grandchildren will not find themselves hurt for Santa's failures on Christmas morning.

So get your shopping done early this year. Try everything out you can, and carefully re-tape the boxes. A broken X-Box on Christmas morning would be a major bummer and could change your kid's relationship with Santa forever.

Chapter 58
The Meaning of a Child

I once heard a minister ask this question: "What has been the most life-changing experience in your life?"

The answer he was expecting, and hoping to receive, was accepting the grace of Christ into our lives. Many people said that, and I agree. But as my mind drifted, as ours usually do during a sermon that has lasts too long and says too little, I thought about other life-changing experiences. There were many: marriage, college, pastoring my first church. Those events caused personal growth and gave me new challenges in life.

However, nothing changed my life as much as when my wife delivered our first child. What a responsibility! I'd never before had to get up twice during the night to feed anything. I knew immediately this child was going to depend upon me for protection, guidance, and love for the rest of my life. I just didn't how realize how much and how often.

I went from knowing the name of Miss November to the name of all the Rugrats in months. Going to a movie became a thing of the past. Things that mattered greatly to me before meant little after his birth.

Even after the child begins to sleep all night, you still worry. The first night our child slept all night, we both got up and crept into the nursery to make sure he was all right. What I didn't know then was I would never have another good night's sleep if I didn't at least think our sons were safe, sound, and happy.

The birth of a child brings families together and makes grown men make funny voices and faces while trying to entertain their grandson. He, somehow, always manages to look like both sides of the family at the same time and even reminds somebody of old dead Uncle Fred, who passed during the Hoover administration from lead poisoning (shot by a jealous girlfriend).

It's no wonder to me that God sent his son to us as a baby, not as a grown man and not with an army of angels. A newborn baby brings hope. They bring peace. They bring both immeasurable joy and occasional great sadness, sometimes at the same time.

A baby born to two young people in a small town on a cold, star-filled night changed the world forever. God's plan for his world became flesh and dwelt among us and offers life-changing grace for us all.

One new baby changed everything!

Chapter 59
Christmas Eve and Gene Simmons

Christmas Eve is an important day in the life of the church. Some of the most moving services I had in my career were Christmas Eve communion services where, in a darkened church, wonderful music was shared, candles were lit, the tree was bright and shining, and everyone was in a festive mood.

It was also an occasion for me to reintroduce myself to those on the church rolls I had not seen since Easter Sunday morning. It was a blessing to have an usher who reminded me of their names when they made their entrance into church. Usually, the conversation went something like this: The usher would gasp and say, "Lord have mercy, look who showed up for church tonight!" I thought it was better to see them twice a year than not see them at all.

Most people who attend Christmas Eve services do not recognize the sacrifice of time and energy that go into those services. A choir and the musicians practiced for weeks and were willing to give up an evening with their families to be there. Communion stewards arrived early to pull out the oldest communion wafers and the store-brand grape juice for folks to enjoy as the body and blood of Christ. Bulletins were printed and ushers were there to hand them out.

It's a concerted effort by all to make such a service happen.

One year I had an idea. I wanted to enable the rest of the church staff to have a night off and be able to be with their families. I wanted the choir to be able to spend the night getting ready for Santa and singing the real songs of Christmas, like "Grandma Got Run over by a Reindeer" and the Chipmunk song at home with their grands. The communion stewards could set the table up early and then decide how they wanted to spend the rest of the evening.

I was going to have a drop-in communion. Between the hours of four and six in the afternoon. the doors would be open, and I encouraged families to come for a moment to take communion as a family together and then go home and enjoy Christmas Eve.

I recorded music on a cassette (which tells you how long ago this was) and had it playing in the background with Christmas hymns while folks came in to kneel together. Small plates with wafers were attached to the communion rails of the church, and all I had to do was serve the juice in the little cups that can get stuck on the end of your tongue if you are trying to get that last drop out.

Everything went well until the tape ended and I had to leave the chancel area and go to the back to turn it over.

As a gift to the church, someone had given us a new table to put the Advent wreath on. Since it was a condemnable act to use fake greens on an Advent wreath, four weeks before, a nice one was made with real pine needles, and it looked great for three weeks. The first Advent candle was short, but I didn't think twice about it.

That is, until I came back into the chancel and a ten-foot-long flame was shooting off the Advent wreath and table. I grabbed a fire extinguisher and blew it all the way off the chancel area near the first pew. The fire was out, and if I was lucky, nobody would notice.

The next family that came in was mine. My wife walked up to me and said, "What the h*#$@! did you do? It looks like a KISS concert in here."

They knelt and took communion, and my wife suggested I change the wafer out. I didn't. I hoped nobody would notice.

After six o'clock came and went, I locked the doors and turned the lights on. Every wafer that had been taken left a clean spot underneath it. Everyone got a powder covered wafer. The sad thing is nobody said a word. They expected the wafers to taste bad, I guess.

The next Christmas Eve, I caught my robe on fire.

Now, the church I serve does not allow me to be near any open flame. On Christmas Eve, we leave the lights on, eat our Hawaiian bread, and use real Welch's grape juice. Some things are just meant to be.

Chapter 60
Home for Christmas

I was driving down the interstate the other day listening to Christmas music. Andy Williams was singing "I'll Be Home for Christmas." That made me start thinking, which was a dangerous thing to do while driving: Just where is home anymore? If I am going home for Christmas, I might need a little help with the directions.

Before my wife and I became traveling nomads for the Methodist Church, we grew up close to each other in Upstate South Carolina. When we got married and she joined me at my first appointment, we still considered home to be where our parents lived. When our children came along several years later, and we had relocated to our next appointment, we made sure our children knew that home was where their Nanas and Poppas lived. Each year at Christmas, we did go home. We loaded our luggage and Santa into our van and went home for Christmas.

Things changed as our children became older and my responsibilities grew during Advent. Our children were fortunate enough to graduate from the same junior and senior high schools. Home for them became Greenville, South Carolina. That's where they made their childhood memories. That's where they found their first girlfriends, played sports, and made lifetime friends among their classmates.

In 2001, I was reappointed to the Charleston area. What a great place to live. We went to Charleston with one son kicking and screaming and one left behind in college. In less than a year, the one in college joined us and we all were together again. They both attended college in Charleston, and we made new friends all over again.

If anyone asked our children where they were from, or where was home, they would reply in unison "Greenville." Yet as time went by, they became intoxicated by the smells and sights of the Lowcountry of South Carolina. Many of their friends are from there, and our grands' other grandparents were from there.

Now we live near North Myrtle Beach. My parents and Margo's dad have passed, and her mom lives in Lyman, South Carolina. Our children now live in Spartanburg County, and our youngest son has a wonderful wife. I want to be home for Christmas, but I don't know where home is anymore. Even though we own a home in Spartanburg that was my parents', and our oldest lives rent-free, we have spent our lives away from there. When we go back to Spartanburg, nothing is the same. The world there changed while we were gone. The town has changed along with us, and it is not home anymore.

Greenville holds nothing for us except memories of our children in simpler times. Our lives are somewhere else now. Time has moved on, and slowly we are, too.

I'll be home for Christmas. Where is home? Home is wherever our family is together. It can be any place we sit down together for a meal. It can be a rental house at Myrtle Beach or Nana's house in Spartanburg. It can be where we are tailgating before another Gamecock victory or where we gathered to lick our wounds together after a disappointing loss.

Home is where love is renewed. It is where new memories are made. It's where family snapshots become family treasures and where the laughter of children drowns out any sorrows we might have brought with us.

We have lived in many houses in many places, but none of them are home to me. Home is, indeed, where the heart is.

I hope you will find home this Christmas, too!

About the Author

The Reverend Dr. Kim Strong is a native of Duncan, South Carolina, and a child of the late Elbert and Ruby Strong. He and his wife, Margo, have been married for forty-four years and have two sons, Matthew and Jonathon, and five grandchildren, Andrew, Kylee, Jonathan, Jacob, and Carolina.

Strong attended James F. Byrnes High School, Wofford College, The Candler School of Theology, and Erskine Theological Seminary. He did postgraduate work at the Harvard Divinity School, The Universidad de Valencia, and the Berklee School of Music. He has served appointments in the South Carolina Conference of The United Methodist Church since 1979.

Strong also served as a military chaplain in the United States Air Force Reserve from 1987-1994, leaving service as a captain. He served on active duty during the first Persian Gulf War.

Strong has written numerous articles for the *South Carolina United Methodist Advocate* and has written an Easter musical, "Are You the King of the Jews?", which has been performed in many churches. He has also written more than fifty songs, some of which he can remember without the words.

Made in the USA
Columbia, SC
27 March 2024

33293318R00086